QUICK & ORGANIZED

HEALTHY

CUISINE

for Busy People

By DONNA SHAFFER CARR

With **DARLENE SUN,** Nutritional Advisor

The Braes Corp.
136 N. Delaware Street
Indianapolis, Indiana 46204

DEDICATIONS

This book is dedicated to the busy working people who not only have no time to study nutrition information, they hardly have time to cook! Hopefully, by using this book, you will be able to quickly prepare healthier, good-tasting food for yourself and those you love.

For Bob
My friend, my love, for whom this project was done

For Ida
Who continually motivated and inspired me

ACKNOWLEGEMENTS

THANKS:

To Estee Lauder - for helping me to develop the professional skills that enabled me to produce this book. For the understanding of people and the sensitivity to their lifestyle needs. And especially for the tremendous programs at Vassar College which stimulated my interest in physical fitness and nutrition.

To my parents, Betty and Ken, who are great cooks and who encouraged my interest in nutrition

To Marsh Inc. for their support

To Jim Strauss, Nancy Weisen and Steve Holman for their cooperation in editing this book

To Abacus computers for their help with the production

INTRODUCTION

When the doctor told my husband "Diet or die" we had to re-think our eating habits. He lost the necessary weight through a medically supervised liquid fast program. But, as with most "diet" programs, it was a short-term solution to a lifetime problem. So....what next? "I don't want to eat rabbit food the rest of my life" was his reaction (a sentiment shared by most of us).

After a 20-year career, which required travelling and great challenges, I had just retired to pursue new interests. Fortunately, this allowed me time to read and research everything I could find on nutrition. The real challange was experimenting with recipes that were healthy, had the great taste we wanted and (for the cook's sake!) were mostly fast and easy to prepare.

After the liquid fast diet, many people gain back one-third of their weight. By simply following the guidelines in this book (making changes in what we ate and watching our portions) my husband and I have both been able to maintain our ideal weights.

Working with a nutritionist is very important. My friend, Pat, who is a physical fitness expert at Vassar introduced me to Darlene Sun. Darlene will earn her Doctorate in Clinical Exercise Physiology and Nutrition in 1990. With her guidance and my "test kitchens" I developed the information in this book.

The purpose of this book is to share basic nutrition information in a way that everyone can easily read and understand. I truly hope that it will make your life easily healthier, too.

Donna Shaffer Carr

CONTENTS

FOREWARD

Several members of my family are overweight and suffer from heart disease. Weight control has been a personal battle for most of my life. I realized that these diseases could be controlled by changing lifestyle habits, such as diet and exercise, and became interested in the preventive aspect of modern chronic diseases.

I've always been interested in humans, animals and the various diseases that may affect them. I pursued a degree in this area and received my B.S. degree in Pathology from the University of Connecticut in 1980. I received my M.A. from the University of Connecticut in Exercise Testing and Training in 1983. I took several nutrition courses in both my undergraduate and graduate programs.

Presently, I am a Doctoral Candidate in Clinical Exercise Physiology with a minor in Nutrition. I plan to complete my Ph.D. in spring 1990. Currently, I am certified as an American College of Sports Medicine Health Fitness Instructor and Exercise Specialist. I have participated in the implementation of the Indiana University Adult fitness Program and have served as Nutrition Coordinator and Counselor. I have also conducted several classes on weight management.

Healthy Cuisine is designed to help individuals prepare low fat, low cholesterol and low sodium meals as part of an overall plan to improve lifestyle habits. Habits can be difficult to change, but hopefully this book will help by providing recipes that are simple, fast and delicious. The information is presented in an abbreviated form for ease of reading. Additional nutrition information and formulated diets can be obtained from a registered dietician in your area. Contact your local hospital or ask your family physician for a referral. The key to success is your commitment and motivation.

Darlene Sun
Nutritional Advisor

ESSENTIAL EXERCISE

ESSENTIAL EXERCISE

Exercise contributes to good health in many ways.

A. The *health related benefits* of exercise include:
1. Improved efficiency of your heart and lungs
2. Burns calories to help in weight loss and weight maintenance
3. May help to control appetite
4. May lower blood pressure
5. Increases good cholesterol and decreases bad cholesterol
6. Helps to decrease depression
7. Improves self image
8. May slow bone loss which occurs in osteoporosis
9. Tones your muscles

B. The best way to improve your heart and to help lose weight with exercise, is through an exercise program consisting of the following components:

1. Type of exercise
Endurance exercises, using large muscle groups, that are continuous and rhythmical in nature. These exercises are termed *aerobic* and examples include:

Walking	Cycling	Aerobic dancing
Jogging	Rowing	Stair-climbing
Swimming	Cross-country skiing	

Choose an exercise you find enjoyable!

2. Frequency
The recommended number of exercise sessions per week: 3 to 5 sessions

3. Duration
Number of minutes at *target heart rate* per session is 20 to 60 minutes

4. Intensity
How hard you exercise should be 60% to 85% of your *maximum heart rate*

ESSENTIAL EXERCISE
(Continued)

5. How to figure your *target* heart rate

First you must know your *maximum* heart rate.

To estimate your *maximum* heart rate, subtract your age from 220

Example: **If you are 40 years old:**

220 - 40 = 180 beats per minute

Determine your *target heart rate range* by multiplying your predicted *maximum* heart rate by 60% to 85%.

Example: **The 40 year old has a *target heart rate range* of**

108 and 153 beats per minute (180 x .60 and 180 x .85)

6. Progression

Start slowly! Start out at 10 minutes, 3 times per week, at 60% of your maximum heart rate. Gradually build up to 20 to 60 minutes.

C. The exercise sessions should consist of 3 phases :

The warm-up   The stimulus or training phase   The cool-down

Warm-up and cool-down

Include stretching and light aerobic activity.

Calisthenics and relaxation exercises may also be incorporated into these phases

The training phase

Consists of the aerobic training activity performed at your *target heart rate*

D. Special caution

See your physician prior to starting an exercise program if:

You are over 35 years of age

Under 35 with any of the conditions listed below

Heart or lung disease	Diabetes
Heart murmur	Obesity
High blood pressure	Bone or joint problems, like arthritis

A family member who had a heart attack before the age of 50

ESSENTIAL NUTRITION

ESSENTIAL NUTRITION INFORMATION

The major frustration most of us have in reading about nutrition is that:

"There seems to be something wrong with everything!"

"The foods I'm supposed to eat are foods I don't want to eat."

The foods recommended in ''HEALTHY *CUISINE*'' are <u>real</u> food and are nutritionally acceptable.

The nutrition information on the following pages has been laid out in a simplified form for easy understanding. The information provided here presents the basics of nutrition. There are many informative books that explain in detail how nutrition affects our health. We encourage you to expand your awareness by reading some of them. They are listed under ''Recommended Reading''.

Regular check-ups with your doctor are essential. You should always be aware of your ''readings'' (blood pressure, cholesterol levels, etc.). The information and recipes in ''HEALTHY *CUISINE*'' are nutritionally acceptable for most people. By achieving a better understanding of nutrition, you can be more in control of your weight and your health.

Not all foods will be considered "healthy" ones. There is room in your diet for some "unhealthy foods", providing they are in limited amounts. The important thing to remember is that your *daily total* of calories should be proportioned as outlined on the next page.

*If you have a specific health problem or are pregnant, be sure to consult your physician and follow the prescribed diet guidelines. The nutrition information provided is for an adult diet.

CALORIES - ENERGY

DON'T FOCUS ON CALORIES ALONE!
CALORIES ARE A *MEASURE* OF ENERGY.

To determine approximately how many calories you may consume each day, multiply your *ideal* weight by 15. The result is your total of daily allowable calories, ***but only if you exercise!*** The American College of Sports Medicine recommends 20-60 minute aerobic exercise periods (such as walking) at least 3 times a week.

Example:
>   125 lbs is your ideal weight
>   125 X 15 = 1875 calories per day

THREE NUTRIENTS THAT PROVIDE CALORIE-ENERGY:
PROTEIN, CARBOHYDRATES and FAT

They yield the following calories:

1 Gram of protein =	**4 Calories**
1 Gram of carbohydrate =	**4 Calories**
1 Gram of fat =	**9 Calories**

Your daily "Calorie Goal"* should be proportioned as:
15% Protein   55% Carbohydrates (or more)   30% Fat (or less)
These are percentages of your total daily calories.

(Alcohol is another source of calories.)

Try to be aware of what *kind* of calories are in the foods you eat.

Examples:

1 Small Potato - Calorie total =				68.0 Calories	
Protein	1.3 Grams x 4	=		5.2 Calories	(7.6%)
Carbohydrates	15.5 Grams x 4	=		62.0 Calories	(92.0%)
Fat	.1 Gram x 9	=		.9 Calories	(1.3%)

1 Slice of Bacon - Calories total =				29.0 Calories	
Protein	1.4 Grams x 4	=		5.6 Calories	(19.0%)
Carbohydrates	.1 Grams x 4	=		.4 Calories	(1.0%)
Fat	2.6 Grams x 9	=		23.4 Calories	(81.0%)

*Recommendation of The American Heart Association and the National Cholesterol Education Program

PROTEIN

INFORMATION

Protein forms the base structure of all cells in the body.

MYTHS: *Protein is good for you, so more is better.*
Protein in excess is needed for exercise.
High protein diets are the best .

TRUTH: *Excess* protein is converted into fat in the body.

Carbohydrates are metabolized more effectively to provide energy for exercise.

Some high protein diets can be dangerous. Too much protein can lead to fluid imbalance and dehydration, especially in the infant and athelete.

THE "BAD NEWS"

High protein diets that include animal products may also be high in cholesterol, total fat and saturated fat.

THE "GOOD NEWS"

Try to get 2/3 of your protein from plants. All necessary protein can come from just plant foods if you combine a grain and vegetable in the same meal.

BEST SOURCES OF LEAN PROTEIN

Soy products (such as Tofu)	Salmon (packed in water)
Tuna (packed in water)	Dry beans and peas
Chicken breast, skinless	Seafood
Turkey breast, skinless	Veal
Skim milk	Lowfat cheese (less than 5 grams of fat per oz.)
Lean red meat	Cottage cheese (less than 5 grams of fat per oz.)
Egg White	Natural peanut butter, no salt or oil added
Dry beans and peas	Yogurt (non-fat or low-fat)

DIETARY FAT

INFORMATION
Fat is the #1 nutritional danger.

There are two types of fat:
Saturated: This type leads to damaged arteries and is predominant in animal foods (meat and dairy products). Saturated fat is the kind of fat that tends to be solid at room temperature.

Unsaturated: This fat is from plants and can be beneficial in lowering blood
Poly- or cholesterol. (The exception is coconut and palm oils) These fats tend
Mono- to be liquid at room temperature.

Ratios: Foods contain a combination of saturated and unsaturated fats. What counts is whether the fat is predominantly saturated or unsaturated. The ratio should be at least **10% polyunsaturated fat, 10% monounsaturated fat, 10% saturated fat.**

THE "BAD NEWS"
Avoid fried foods

The dangers of fat in relation to heart disease:
High intakes of saturated fat can raise blood cholesterol levels and contribute to atherosclerosis and coronary heart disease.
The dangers of fat in relation to cancer:
Cancers most strongly linked to a high-fat diet are those of the colon, breast, prostate, ovary and uterus.
The dangers of fat in relation to obesity:
Excessive fat intake is one cause of obesity. Obesity itself is a risk factor for coronary heart disease.

THE "GOOD NEWS"
Decreasing total and saturated fat intake can cause a major drop in blood cholesterol.

BEST SOURCES FOR FOODS LOW IN DIETARY FAT
Skim milk	Seafood
White meat poultry	Fruits and vegetables
Beans	Whole grain breads

CARBOHYDRATES

INFORMATION

There are **good and bad carbohydrates.** This is a comparison of what you should eat vs. what you probably already eat:

	Recommended % of Calories	Typical diet % of Calories
Good Carbohydrates		
"Complex Carbohydrates"		
(Starches)	48	28
"Natural Sugars"		
(Fruit, milk, yogurt)		
Bad Carbohydrates		
Refined and processed sugars		
(This includes sugars added to	10	18
processed foods)		

Complex carbohydrates provide energy and fiber as well as other nutrients such as thiamin, niacin and iron. This is why they are so highly recommended.

Refined sugars supply little else but calories. They are considered "empty calories." Brown sugar, "raw" sugar and honey are no better nutritionally than regular sugar.

Fructose is a natural sugar found in fruit and is absorbed by the body more slowly than sugar. It can be used in some recipes in place of regular sugar. While fructose is still considered "added sugar," it is sweeter than regular sugar so less of it is needed.

THE "BAD NEWS"

Sugar's "empty calories" consumed in excess may contribute to weight gain and obesity.

THE "GOOD NEWS"

Reasons to eat more **Complex Carbohydrates:**

1. Each gram of complex carbohydrate supplies only four calories, while fat supplies nine.
2. They are filling because they provide more food bulk.

3. Complex carbohydrates are "nutrient dense." They contain a high nutrients-per-calorie ratio.

BEST SOURCES

Cereals	Rice
Whole grain breads	Barley
Beans	Pasta
Popcorn	Vegetables
Fruits	

DIETARY FIBER

INFORMATION

Nationally, we average an intake of 11 grams of fiber a day, when we **need** to average **20 to 30 grams daily.** People with digestive problems should consult their physician about dietary fiber.

Soluble fiber: is a gel-forming fiber that has been shown to lower blood cholesterol when consumed with a low-fat diet. Sources of **soluble fiber** are **fruit, vegetables, oats and barley.**

Insoluble fiber: is a bulk-forming fiber that helps the rate of food through the digestive tract. Sources of **insoluble fiber** are **whole grains** like **whole wheat** and **whole rye.**

Bran: Fiber is found in the **bran** of the grain, which is the protective coating around the grain kernel.

THE "BAD NEWS"

More fiber is very important. Although, too much fiber can result in gastrointestinal discomfort and inhibit the body's absoption of vitamins and minerals. Fiber intake should be increased gradually. Remember to try to balance your foods!

THE "GOOD NEWS"

A healthy fiber-rich diet can lower blood cholesterol and may reduce the risk of developing colon cancer.

BEST SOURCES

Fiber-rich foods that are cancer-preventers:

Broccoli	Carrots	Cabbage family (Turnips, kale)
Cauliflower	Vitamin C foods	Brussels sprouts
Wheat bran	Whole grain breads	Vegetables with skins

Fiber-rich foods that are cardiovascular helpers:

Oat bran	Grapefruit	Dried beans, prunes and dates	
Broccoli	Bananas	Vegetables with skins	
Apples	Carrots	Barley	Nectarines
Oats	Asparagus	Blackberries	Green peppers

BLOOD CHOLESTEROL

INFORMATION
There are *two* types of cholesterol: **Good & Bad!**

Bad cholesterol:
>Known as **LDL**, carries cholesterol through the blood to tissues in the body. This is the cholesterol that buildsup on artery walls and hardens arteries.

Good cholesterol;
>Known as **HDL**, acts as scavengers, grabbing up cholesterol, carrying it away from the arteries to the liver where it is destroyed.

The body actually *produces* cholesterol in the liver.

THE "BAD NEWS"
Bad cholesterol is promoted by:
>**Smoking   Obesity**
>**High saturated fat intake & possibly dietary cholesterol**
>**Stress**   (Stress causes the liver to produce more bad cholesterol)

THE "GOOD NEWS"
The "Cholesterol Fighters":
>**Monounsaturated fats (Olive, Peanut and Canola oils)**
>(Lower the bad cholesterol while maintaining the good)
>**Soluble fiber - found in fruits , vegetables & oats**
>(Helps to lower blood cholesterol)

BEST SOURCES TO CONTROL BLOOD CHOLESTEROL

Oat bran	Dried beans	Barley	Carrots
Grapefruit	Fresh fruit	Olive oil	Yogurt (non-fat)
Soybean	Fish		

DIETARY CHOLESTEROL

INFORMATION

The liver can produce all the cholesterol the body needs. Your maximum intake should be **no more than 300 mg daily.**

Dietary cholesterol is *not* the same as blood cholesterol.

THE "BAD NEWS"

Be careful of "No cholesterol" claims on grocery items. They mean **no** *dietary cholesterol* and can be misleading. Check the label for fat content. The food may not contain *dietary cholesterol,* **but if it contains more than 30% fat and the ratios of** *saturated* **fat are high, the** *saturated fat content* **can** *increase* **blood cholesterol !**

THE "GOOD NEWS"

Cutting back on your cholesterol intake may help lower your blood cholesterol. Foods high in cholesterol may also be high in saturated fat, which *does* increase your blood cholesterol. The majority of your calories should come from starchy, fibrous foods which do not contain cholesterol anyway.

Shellfish (shrimp, lobster, etc.) are high in dietary cholesterol but very low in fat. Shellfish *are* acceptable, but no more than once a week. *Surimi* or *imitation crab* is actually pressed whitefish so you may enjoy it as often as you like.

BEST FOODS

Fresh fruit   Vegetables   Oats

FOODS TO AVOID

Whole eggs (no more than 4 eggs a week, including eggs in baked foods)
Whole cream
Organ meats (liver, brains, etc.)
Whole milk dairy products
Cream cheese (including "Neufchatel" cheese)
Coconut and palm oils

CALCIUM

INFORMATION

Calcium is important for teeth, bones, muscle contraction and blood clotting. Eight out of ten women do not consume enough calcium. At age 35 everyone starts losing bone tissue.

Our body's ability to absorb calcium decreases with age, therefore it is important to get an adequate intake. The most recent Recommended Dietary Allowance is 800 mg per day for women 25 years of age or older and 1200 mg per day for women under 25.

THE "BAD NEWS"

Osteoporosis "High-risk" women
Underweight
Heavy alcohol users
Smokers
Family history of osteoporosis
Caucasion or Oriental women

Calcium "Busters"
High protein diets
Smoking
Stress
Alcohol
Very low calories diets

Other low-calcium dangers
High blood pressure
Peridontal bone loss

THE "GOOD NEWS"

Calcium "Boosters"
Vitamin D
Protein
Lactose (milk sugar)
Sunshine

BEST SOURCES

Skim milk   Salmon   Kale   Turnips and mustard greens
Dried beans   Broccoli   Tofu   Yogurt (low-fat or non-fat)
Parmesan, Gruyere, Mozzarella and Monterey Jack cheeses, low-fat
Salmon, Sardines (with soft, edible bones)

SODIUM

INFORMATION

The average American consumes **3600 to 6000 mg** of sodium per day. The Food and Nutrition Board of the National Academy of Sciences recommends **1100 to 3300** mg per day.

Foods high in sodium do not always taste salty. Know your nutrient facts.

THE "BAD NEWS"

Excess sodium may contribute to high blood pressure, kidney disease and calcium loss.

Where excess sodium is found in the average diet:
Added in cooking or at the table   36%-42%

THE "GOOD NEWS"

Increasing intakes of calcium, potassium can reduce the effect of sodium in the body.

FOODS TO AVOID

Packaged foods	Olives	Table salt
Pickles	Soy sauce, regular	Caviar
Ham	Hot dogs	Boullion (regular)
Canned soups (read the label)	Worchestershire sauce (regular)	

High-salt snack foods (Potato chips, tortilla chips etc.)

IRON

INFORMATION

Iron is important for the transporting of oxygen in the blood and enzyme functions.

Women on low-calorie diets generally do not get enough iron. Low iron levels can result in anemia. The Recommended Dietary Allowance for women is 15 mg per day and for men is 10 mg.

Symptoms of iron-deficiency:
> Muscle weakness
> Decreased exercise tolerance
> Poor job performance
> Fatigue

THE "BAD NEWS"

Avoid:
Aspirin

THE "GOOD NEWS"

Helpful in building iron in the body:
Vitamin C (eaten with an iron source)
Cooking with an iron skillet
Fish, poultry and red meat protein

BEST SOURCES

Yeast	Spinach	Lean red meat
Molasses	Wheat germ	Oysters
Fish	Pine nuts	Potatoes (with skin)
Sardines	Dried apricots	Prune juice
Broccoli	Poultry	Whole enriched grains

POTASSIUM

INFORMATION

Potassium is a mineral found in the body and in most foods. Potassium plays a major role in neurological transmission and muscle contractions. A deficiency of potassium can lead to muscular weakness and heart abnormalities.

Deficiencies of potassium may be a result of heavy sweating, starvation, diarrhea, and the use of certain diuretics.

Your daily intake should be between 1500mg and 5000 mg.

THE "BAD NEWS"

Excess potassium can cause heart abnormalities as well as intestinal irritation. *Avoid potassium supplements* unless prescribed by your physician. Salt substitutes are made by replacing the sodium with potassium and may not be recommended for people with heart or kidney disease.

"THE GOOD NEWS"

Adequate potassium intake can be obtained by consuming the foods listed under "Best Sources". Many of these foods are also high in complex carbohydrates and low in sodium. Atheletes exercising in the heat will want to consume 5 to 8 servings of these foods per day.

A high dietary potassium intake may lower blood pressure in those individuals with high blood pressure. A relationship has been shown between high potassium intake and lower incidence of stroke.

BEST SOURCES

Fresh lean red meat	Lima Beans	Dried beans, peas and lentils
Potatoes	Bananas	Brussel sprouts
Broccoli	Asparagus	Cantaloupe
Haddock	Cauliflower	Citrus fruits and juices
Tomatoes	Carrots	Tomato juice, low-salt
Canned salmon low-salt	Canned tuna low-salt	Peanut butter, low-salt

"TIPS FOR GETTING SMARTER"

TIPS FOR "GETTING SMARTER"

1. "Diet is a four-letter word!"

Don't concentrate on just calories. Don't be preoccupied with constantly being "on a diet". Eating healthier and watching your *portion sizes* should give you long-term control of your weight.

2. After-work "nibbles"

This is the worst time of the day. If you are at work or travelling - snack on an apple or low-salt pretzels *or* drink a large glass of water (which will make you feel full and drinking more water is healthy for your system). If you are at home - have fresh fruit, cereal or try the "Tuna Dip" or"Salmon Dip" recipes on low-salt crackers. Air-popped popcorn is terrific.

3. Substitutes for "junk food"

Try "white cheddar popcorn", air-popped popcorn or rice crunch crackers in different flavors. These are great tasting snacks and better for you than the fried, salted snacks you may be eating. But remember to eat just *one* portion.

4. Get a food scale!

In many recipes you will need to measure ingredients in ounces. You may also want to weigh your portions to verify your intake.

5. Balance your meals

Carbohydrates and fiber are so important to your health and weight control and are easily achieved if you make sure that your meals are well balanced. Try to have fruit with every meal and in the place of junk food. Dinner should consist of 3 ounces of meat or pasta, fresh vegetables (properly prepared), rice or potatoe, salad, bread and fruit.

6. Time

Long day? Pick a 20-30 minute recipe. You can fix dinner in less time than it takes to drive to a restaurant! Many recipes are 30 minutes or less. Most are less than 1 hour. Other recipes have been simplified from the originals and are well worth the extra minutes. Save time by using a microwave to thaw frozen foods.

7. Preparation time work tip

After selecting your recipe, take a minute to pull out all your ingredients and begin thawing any frozen foods needed. Your work will be easier and go faster if everything is in front of you. Also, there is less chance of overlooking an ingredient.

TIPS FOR "GETTING SMARTER"
(Continued)

8. Utilizing your cooking time

If the food you're preparing requires extended baking or simmering time, use it to your advantage. Use it to prepare the side dishes, clean up the dirty dishes (so there are fewer to do when you've finished) or just relax!

9. Planning your time

Your schedule is often unpredictable, if you are like most of us. But whenever you can, give some thought to what you would like to prepare for the week ahead. Nutritionists recommend that you set up a "menu" for each of your 3 meals by day. If this is not possible, do try to have a general idea of meals you will be making on days when you can. You will be amazed at how planning ahead makes eating at home easier!

10. Fresh vs frozen..."freeze your needs!"

You will find it very helpful to keep a basic stock of **meats, vegetables** and **fruit** in your freezer. Fresh foods taste best, of course, and you should try to use fresh whenever possible. But frozen foods are very good, too, and are so very convenient. Frozen foods can be thawed in minutes in your microwave.

11. Non-stick pans

Always use non-stick pans. You will seldom need to use oils or margarine. Meats will brown in their own juices. Use a vegetable cooking spray to coat pans for baking and frying.

12. Adding your "vegetable touches"

The most important point is that your food is prepared to your personal taste. If you like extra vegetables like onion, green peppers, mushrooms, whatever, feel free to modify the recipes to your taste, using the acceptable foods.

13. A "Running Grocery List"

Your *Pantry Guide* is a great list of basics that supply you with most everything you will need for any recipe. As you use products from your pantry basics, write them down on a *Running Grocery List*. Then when you make your trip to the grocery, you will know exactly what you need.

TIPS FOR "GETTING SMARTER"

14. Margarines

Buy margarines with at least a 2 to 1 ratio of unsaturated fats over saturated fats. Choose soft tub margarines instead of stick margarines. (Some stick margarine is hydrogenated, meaning the fat content will be higher in saturated fats.) Be sure to read the labels.

15. Flours

Whole grain flours are better for you than bleached flour, but generally cannot be used alone in baking. Select white *unbleached* flour and try to incorporate some wheat or rye into your favorite recipes.

16. Grill, broil and barbecue

Cooking any meat using any of these methods is fast, easy and adds a wonderful flavor. Grilling is healthy because some of the fats drain off while cooking. Baste with low-sodium worchestershire sauce and lemon juice. Avoid regular barbecue sauces as they are generally high in sugar and salt.

17. Tools for new cooks

Measuring   Get **2** sets of measuring cups and measuring spoons: *When working with these, use **1** set for **dry ingredients** and use **1** set for **wet ingredients.** This simplifies your utensil inventory and makes for fewer dirty dishes!

Pans   You need one large skillet, one small skillet; saucepans in small medium and large sizes, a glass or porcelain casserole dish, souffle dish and pans in small, medium and large sizes for microwaving. Individual glass baking dishes are handy, also.

Mixing bowls &   One set of glass bowls and one set of metal or porcelain bowls deep
Electric Mixer   enough to use with an electric mixer.

Sharp knives &   A set of small, medium and large knives kept sharp help greatly.
Food processor   Having a food processor or blender makes fine chopping easier

Microwave   A small microwave helps to thaw and cook foods quickly.

Utensils   Wooden spoons, rubber scrapers, spatulas, whisk, slotted spoon.

"LIVABLE SUGGESTIONS"
FOR RESTAURANTS

"LIVABLE SUGGESTIONS"
for RESTAURANTS

BEST	LIMIT

BREAKFAST:

Fresh fruits and juices

Egg Substitutes (they *are* good!)   Whole eggs
(If these are not available, eat only the
egg white)

Whole grain breads, bagels or   Sweet rolls, doughnuts,
English muffin   croissants

Margarine, in small amounts,   Butter, cream cheese
served on the side. (Or try a teaspoon
of jelly instead)

Hot cereals: oatmeal, oat bran
Cold cereals: shredded wheat, bran

Skim milk   Whole milk, cream

Canadian bacon (occasionally)   Bacon, sausage

LUNCH:

Pasta with tomato sauce   Cream sauces

Salad (with dressing on the side: Salads with cheese, bacon,
low-cal vinegar & oil, lemon juice)   eggs, meat or croutons

Tuna, chicken or turkey salads   Smoked, cured & or
(with minimum mayonnaise)   processed meats

41

"LIVABLE SUGGESTIONS"
for Restaurants
(Continued)

	BEST	LIMIT
LUNCH:		
	Sliced turkey or chicken sandwich	Any fried foods
	Broth soups (may be high in sodium)	Cream soups
	Low-fat cottage cheese	
	Pizza (with vegetable toppings)	
	Grilled chicken sandwich (without skin)	Hot dogs
DRINKS:	Juices, diet sodas, skim milk decaffeinated coffee, mineral water, or Sparklers (fruit juice & mineral water)	Sodas with caffeine & sugar Whole milk, non-dairy creamers
DINNER:		
APPETIZERS:	Clams, scallops, oysters (steamed or raw, no sauce)	
	Fresh vegetables or fruits	Cream soups
	Brothy or gazpacho soup (may be high in sodium)	French onion soup
DRINKS:	Same as lunch	
	Alcohol (if you prefer) - please limit to: White wine (8 oz glass) Light beer (24 oz)	

"LIVABLE SUGGESTIONS"
for Restaurants
(Continued)

DINNER:

BEST	LIMIT
"Share" a dinner with a friend (Your meat portion should be 3-4 oz., order extra vegetables)	
Chicken or turkey (Skinless, white meat)	Duck or any game meat
Fish: sole, halibut, salmon, pike, swordfish, tuna, roughy	Lobster
Lean beef: sirloin, round, flank steaks	Prime rib, spareribs, corned beef brisket; any meat marbled in fat
Lean pork, veal, lamb	Organ meats, pot pies
Brown, wild and white rice	Fried potatoes or potatoes in cream sauce
Baked potato topped with: cottage cheese, margarine or yogurt	Pickled vegetables
Steamed or stir-fried vegetables	Vegetables in cheese, cream or butter sauces
Linguine with clam, marsala or marinara sauce	

Order meats that are grilled, broiled, baked roasted, stir-fried, poached or steamed. Always ask what the food is cooked in. Broiled entrees are sometimes basted with fat. Ask to have your entree prepared without added fat or request the preparation with vegetable oils or margarine.

43

"LIVABLE SUGGESTIONS"
for Restaurants
(Continued)

	BEST	LIMIT
DESSERTS:		
	Fresh fruit	Cakes, cookies and brownies
	Frozen yogurt	Ice cream
	Sherbet, fruit ice, ice milk	Custard
	Angel food cake	
	Oatmeal-raisin cookies, natural peanut butter cookies (restaurant cookies tend to be high in fat, sugar)	
	Pretzels (low-salt)	Potato chips
	Popcorn (air-popped)	
		Macadamia nuts; salted or oiled nuts
	Dry roasted peanuts, almonds	

Whenever possible, carry a small shaker of a dry butter substitute with you. This is a terrific tasting substitute for butter and it has a slightly salty taste, too. You can order your food with minimal seasoning and use this product instead. It is a good all-round flavor enhancer!

THE PANTRY GUIDE

"YOU'VE GOT WHAT IT TAKES!"
A Pantry Guide

About the *Pantry Guide*

This guide makes it easier for those spur-of-the-moment decisions to cook. They are listed as *Pantry Basics* (for foods you can have on hand any time) and *Perishables* (for those foods you will need weekly).

Product availability

Many major food companies have recently introduced low-fat, low-salt products. So you can easily find healthier products at any major grocery.

Buying the right foods

Read the nutrition labels! Many products produced in the U. S. have nutrient information and ingredients listed. Look for:

1. **Fat content** - The "polyunsaturated" or "monounsaturated" fats must be proportionately two to one over "saturated" fats. A higher ratio is better.

2. **Coconut &** - These oils are saturated and tend to increase blood cholesterol.
   Palm oils

3. **Sodium** - Excess sodium is a risk factor for blood pressure. Beware of these terms on food labels: *salt, brine, MSG, soy sauce, boullion, sodium compounds.*

4. **Cholesterol** - "Low" cholesterol claims on package labels do not mean that the product is low in saturated or total fat, which can cause higher levels of blood cholesterol.

5. **"Light"** - Lighter than what? The product may contain less fat than the original, but does not necessarily mean it is nutritionally OK. Be sure to read the label for cholesterol and fat content. Notice the amount of the *serving size.*

6. **Oat bran** - Everything seems to have oat bran in it today. Be sure to read the labels. Some products featuring oat bran have high fat and sodium content.

Also avoid products containing: *hydrogenated fats and oils, cocoa butter, animal fats, egg yolks and egg yolk solids, powdered whole milk solids, milk chocolate.*

"YOU'VE GOT WHAT IT TAKES!"
A Pantry Guide
(Continued)

Buying the right foods
(Continued)

Meats	*Red meats* - have the meat counter trim all visible fat (or you can do this yourself). Choose only *lean* cuts such as: *sirloin, round, chuck, flank and veal.* Occasionally try *lamb* and *very lean pork.*
	Poultry - have the meat counter remove the skin (or you can do this yourself). Choose only white meat, which is lower in cholesterol than dark meat. Avoid self - basting poultry. Most of these are injected with saturated fat.
Packaged or processed food	"Convenience" foods are often higher in fat and sodium. Be sure to read the labels.
Margarines	Read the labels to be sure the Polyunsatured and Monounsaturated fats are at least twice the content of saturated fat.
Soy sauce and Worchestershire sauce	These are very high is sodium. Read the labels for low-sodium versions. The low-sodium types add great flavor in recipes.
Oils	The best oils to use are Olive, Canola and Peanut oils. These are monounsaturated. They are generally used for frying, although Canola can be used in place of regular vegetable oils due to it's mild taste. Other good oils are Sesame, Safflower, Corn and Soybean.
Cooking spray	Whenever possible, use non-stick pans and vegetable cooking spray. It is easier and tastier than you may think.
Boullion	Boullions are very high in sodium. If possible, make your own stock. There *are* new boullions on the market that are low in sodium.

THE PANTRY GUIDE

Non-Perishables

Pantry Basics

Almonds, sliced
Artichokes, jar or can
Baking powder (low-sodium)
Baking soda
Boullion,**Herb-Ox** ⑧ low sodium(beef, chicken)
Brown sugar
Brown Sugar Twin ®
Butter Buds®
Cocoa (unsweetened)
Cooking spirits (Brandy, sherry, vermouth, white wine)
Cooking spray (vegetable base)
Cornstarch
Dijon mustard
Dry milk, non-fat
Evaporated skim milk
Extract, almond
Extract, vanilla
Flours (Unbleached white, wheat)
Graham crackers, oat bran
Grains (White long-grain, brown, and wild rice; barley)
Honey
Hot sauce
Horseradish
Jellies (**Simply Fruit** ™)
Ketchup, no salt added
Lemon juice
Mushrooms, jar
Oats
Oat Bran
Onions
Oils (Olive and /or canola; sesame or safflower or corn)
Pasta (Shell, spiral, spinach fettucini, spaghetti)
Parmesan cheese, dry, grated
Peanut butter, natural, no salt or oils added

Spices & Herbs

Allspice
Basil
Bay leaves
Cayenne pepper
Celery seed
Chives
Cinnamon
Cloves
Curry
Garlic powder
Ginger
Marjoram
Mustard, dry
Nutmeg
Oregano
Paprika
Parsley
Pepper, black
Pepper, white
Rosemary
Sage
Sesame seeds
Thyme

*Make a combination of your favorite herbs to use for seasoning instead of salt!

THE PANTRY GUIDE

Non-Perishables
(Continued)

Pantry Basics
Potatoes
Raisins
Romano cheese, dry, grated
Salmon, canned in water
Salt
Soy sauce, low sodium
Sugar
Sweet 'n Low ®
Tomato paste, no salt added
Tomato sauce, no salt added
Tomatoes, whole, canned
Tuna (Albacore), canned in water
Vinegars (Balsamic, raspberry, white wine)
Wheat germ
White grape juice
Worchestershire sauce, low sodium
Yeast

Frozen foods
Egg substitute (**Egg Beaters** ® **or Egg Scramblers** ®)
Fruit, in bags (Raspberries, blueberries, strawberries)
Vegetables, preferably in bags (Green beans, peas, broccoli, spinach)
Meats (Chicken breast, turkey breast, veal cutlets, extra-lean gound beef, sirloin steak, chuck)
Fish (Surimi [imitation crab], salmon, sole, grouper, swordfish, halibut)
Orange juice
Cheese pizza (For when you *really* don't want to cook!)

Perishables
Dairy
Cheese, low-fat (Cheddar, monterey jack, Mozzarella)
Eggs (For the egg white)
Margarine (**Fleischmann's Light** ®**, Promise Light** ® or **Mazola 100% Corn Oil** ®)
Mayonnaise (**Miracle Whip Light** ®)
Skim milk

THE PANTRY GUIDE

Perishables
(Continued)

Dairy
Yogurt, **Dannon**® (Plain non-fat and vanilla low-fat)

Produce
Carrots
Celery
Garlic
Green Onions
Lemons
Lettuce
Mushrooms
Tomatoes

Fresh vegetables: Your choice
Fresh fruit: Your choice
Bread: Whole wheat bread, wheat English muffins, wheat or rye bagels, French, sourdough

Brand Name Sources

Brown Sugar Twin ®	Alberto Culver Foods Service
Butter Buds®	Cumberland Packing Corp.
Dannon ®	Dannon
Egg Beaters ®	Fleischmann's
Fleischmann's Light ®	Fleischmann's
Mazola 100% Corn Oil ®	Best Foods Corp.
Miracle Whip Light	Kraft Foods
Sweet 'n Low ®	Cumberland Packing Corp.
Promise Light ®	Lever Bros.
Scramblers ®	Morningstar Farms
Simply Fruit ™	The J M Smucker Co.

THE MENU GUIDE

THE MENU GUIDE

About the Menu Guide
Use this "Menu Guide" to help plan:

Time   The "Menu Guide" indicates the amount of preparation time and total time needed for each recipe. You may choose a 20 minute recipe or plan the day before for marinating.

Calories   The calories for each recipe are noted to help quickly plan the entree, vegetable and even a dessert that totally fits into your daily calorie allowance. Remember, though, calories do not tell the whole story.

Ingredients   Next to each recipe there is a notation of the major food items needed that you may not normally have on hand. This enables you to know at a glance if you have what it takes to make that specific recipe.

This is helpful for spur-of-the-moment cooking as well as planning your weekly grocery shopping. (If you keep a stock of the foods listed on the *Pantry Guide* and you will usually have what you need!)

THE MENU GUIDE

BREAKFASTS AND BREADS

Page	Recipes	Time	Calories	"Extra Ingredient Needs"
73	Quick Carbohydrate Breakfast	10M	140	Apples, yogurt, wheat germ, oats
74	Breakfast casserole	35M	132	Monterey jack cheese, tomatoes, wheat bread
75	Vegetable Omelet	20M	150	Monterey jack cheese, spinach, tomatoes, sherry
76	Apple-Cinnamon Bread Pudding	1Hr	95	Apples, wheat bread, cheese, milk
77	French Toast	15M	186	Bread, yogurt, white grape juice, strawberries or blueberries
78	Pancakes	15M	134	Strawberries, yogurt, flour
79	Wheat Biscuits	40M 30M prep.	47	Plain yogurt nonfat, buttermilk, flour
80	"Indiana Scones"	45M 25M prep.	84	Buttermilk, eggs, milk
81	Apricot Tea Ring	2 Hr 30M prep.	126	Dried apricots, yeast, almonds
82	Dinner Rolls	3.5Hr 25M prep.	85	Yeast, milk, eggs, egg substitute
83	Cheese Dinner Rolls	2.2Hr 30M prep.	7	Yeast, monterey jack cheese, yogurt, cheddar cheese
84	Whole Wheat Oatmeal Bread	4.2Hr 30M prep.	84	Yeast, wheat germ, yogurt, honey

THE MENU GUIDE
(Continued)

SAUCES, TOPPINGS, DIPS & DRESSINGS

Page	Recipes	Time	Calories	"Extra Ingredient Needs"
87	Dijon Salad Dressing	15M	65	Balsamic or raspberry vinegar, dijon mustard, sesame oil, onion, canola oil
88	Yogurt Dressing	10M	9	Plain yogurt, worchestershire sauce, low sodium
89	Coleslaw	5M	55	Buttermilk, shredded cabbage, yogurt, horseradish, light mayonnaise
90	A Dip for all Reasons	5M	19	Plain yogurt, onion, chives
91	Tuna Dip	10M	56	Canned albacore tuna in water, yogurt, light mayonnaise
92	Salmon Dip	10M	56	Canned salmon, light mayonnaise, nonfat yogurt
93	Cheese Sauce	10M	45	Monterey jack cheese, milk, dry milk, Butter Buds
94	Chocolate Sauce	10M	44	Cocoa, instant coffee, milk
95	Streusel Topping	5M	40	Brown sugar, canola oil, coca, flour, cinnamon
96	Coffee Creamer	5M	10	Dry coffee creamer, nonfat dry milk
97	Yogurt Cream Cheese	6-8Hr 15M prep.	70	Plain or vanilla yogurt, cheesecloth
98	Whipped Topping	5M	14	Egg whites, vanilla yogurt, sugar

SOUPS & STEWS

101	Crab Bisque	20M	115	Imitation crab, onions, potatoes, milk, sherry
102	Gazpacho	35M	58	Tomatoes, vinegar, canned tomatoes, cucumber, celery, horseradish
103	Vichyssoise	50M 20M prep.	148	Potatoes, green onion, bacon, celery, chicken broth
104	Creamy Mushroom Soup	45M 20M prep.	93	Potatoes, beef broth, carrot, sherry, mozzarella
105	Heart meat & Pasta Soup	45M 15M prep.	110	Turkey sausage or lean ground beef, red wine, spinach, fettucini, carrot, celery
106	Corn Chowder	1 1/2 Hr 15M prep.	125	Frozen corn, bacon, celery, carrot, potatoes, milk
107	Chicken Noodle Soup	3Hr 15M prep.	73	Chicken breast, eggless noodles
108	Chicken Stew	1 1/4 Hr 25M prep.	160	Chicken breast, carrot, celery, chicken broth, peas, green beans, potatoes

THE MENU GUIDE
(Continued)

VEGETABLES & GRAINS

Page	Recipes	Time	Calories	"Extra Ingredient Needs"
111	Stir-fried Vegetables	25M	78	Sesame oil, sesame seeds, pea pods, bean sprouts, broccoli, carrot, celery
112	Corn on the Cob	15M	91	Corn on the cob, Butter Buds
113	Vegetables in Cheese Sauce	15M	47	"Cheese Sauce" recipe, broccoli or asparagus
114	Sesame Broccoli	10M	82	Broccoli, sesame oil, sesame seeds
115	Green Beans Almondine	20M	83	Green beans, almonds, mushrooms
116	Green Beans & Rice	25M 5M prep.	187	Rice, green beans, monterey jack cheese, milk
117	Summer Squash Cakes	15M	68	Summer squash, onion, parmesan, egg substitute
118	Spinach Souffle	25M	67	Spinach, onion, parmesan, romano cheese
119	Spinach Quiche	1Hr 25M prep.	157	Spinach, cheddar cheese, half & half, milk
120	Special Spinach	15M	97	Spinach, white wine, chicken boullion, bacon
121	Tomatoes Provencale	10M	43	Tomatoes, bread crumbs, parmesan
122	Vegetable-Cheese Pie	45M 25M prep.	109	Tomatoes, ricotta & mozzarella cheeses, carrots, green beans, cottage cheese
123	Brown & Wild Rice	40M 5 M prep.	78	Brown and wild rice, chicken boullion
124	Baked Potatoes Light	45M 5M prep.	70	Potatoes, cottage cheese, chives
125	Fluffy Twice-Baked Potatoes	40M 15M prep.	98	Potatoes, milk, yogurt, monterey jack cheese, lowfat cheddar cheese
126	Mashed Potatoes	20M	129	Potatoes, yogurt, milk, Butter Buds
127	Creamed Potatoes & Peas	50M 20M prep.	160	Potatoes, peas, carrots, yogurt, dry mustard

THE MENU GUIDE
(Continued)

VEGETABLES & GRAINS(Continued)

Page	Recipes	Time	Calories	"Extra Ingredient Needs"
128	Gourmet Potatoes	45M 20M prep.	231	Potatoes, chicken boullion, yogurt, almonds, monterey jack cheese, mushrooms
129	Crispy-fried Potatoes	20M	127	Potatoes, green peppers, onion, parmesan cheese
130	Stir-fried Rice	15M	164	Rice, mushrooms, zucchini, sesame seeds, chicken boullion, waterchestnuts
131	Barley with Vegetables	50M 15M prep.	89	Barley, green onions, green beans, white wine, mushrooms

PASTA

Page	Recipe	Time	Calories	"Extra Ingredient Needs"
135	Pasta Salad	30M 15M prep.	240	Spiral pasta, balsamic or raspberry vinegar, tomatoes, onion, parmesan
136	Spaghetti with Meat Sauce	45M 15M prep.	256	Ground beef or turkey, canned tomatoes, canned tomatoes, tomato paste, spaghetti
137	New York Pasta	20M	238	Angel hair pasta, tomatoes, recipe for cheese
138	Pasta with Crab & Vegetables	25M	387	Spiral pasta, white wine, imitation crab, peas, tomatoes, mushrooms
139	Pasta in Tomato Wine Sauce	30M	270	Fettucini, red wine, romano, parmesan, onion
140	Lasagna	1 1/2Hr 45M prep.	268	Lasagna noodles, ground beef or turkey, canned tomatoes, romano, ricotta, parmesan, mozzarella, cottage cheese
141	Mini Pizzas	15M	189	Canned tomatoes, tomato paste, mozzarella, english muffins
142	Easy Cheese Pizza	20M	274	Frozen cheese pizza, green pepper, artichokes

THE MENU GUIDE
(Continued)

POULTRY

Page	Recipes	Time	Calories	"Extra Ingredient Needs"
145	Oven-fried Chicken	1Hr 10M prep.	167	Chicken breasts, corn flakes, almonds
146	Chicken Stir-fry	30M	264	Chicken breasts, carrots, celery, sherry, bean sprouts, green beans, waterchestnuts
147	Coq au Vin	1Hr 15M prep.	189	Chicken breasts, chicken boullion, bacon, wine
148	Chicken Florentine	45M 15M prep.	273	Chicken breasts, spinach, mozzarella, bacon
149	Chicken Almondine	20M	141	Chicken or turkey breasts, brandy, almonds, milk, mushrooms
150	Arroz con Pollo	1Hr 15M prep.	222	Chicken breasts, rice, tomato sauce, peas, capers, green peppers
151	Fajitas in a Pita	30M	431	Chicken breasts, wheat pitas, yogurt, lettuce, cheddar cheese, white wine, tomatoes, salsa
152	Oriental Chicken with Rice	25M 15M prep.	177	Chicken breasts, chicken boullion, rice, carrots, peas, sherry
153	Chicken Teriyaki Broil	30M 10M prep.	248	Chicken breasts, sherry, pineapple juice
154	Baked Chicken	55M 15M prep.	261	Chicken breasts, milk, egg substitute
155	Chicken & Crab Rolls	45M 30M prep.	265	Chicken breasts, almonds, imitation crab, parmesan or blue cheese, plain yogurt
156	Island Chicken	1Hr 15M prep.	196	Chicken breasts, onion, mustard, worchestershire sauce, low sodium
157	Turkey-Cheese Crescents	45M 20M prep.	234	Turkey or veal cutlets, monterey jack cheese, milk, almonds, oat bran
158	Turkey Sloppy Joes	1 1/4 Hr 15M prep.	144	Ground turkey or extra lean ground beef, celery, tomato sauce, ketchup, hamburger buns

THE MENU GUIDE
(Continued)

FISH

Page	Recipes	Time	Calories	"Extra Ingredient Needs"
161	Japanese Crab Cakes	20M	151	Imitation crab, peas, green pepper
162	Crab & Artichokes	35M 20M prep.	171	Imitation crab, artichoke hearts, sherry
163	Sole with Vegetables	50M 15M prep.	195	Sole, tomatoes, monterey jack cheese, chicken boullion
164	Caribbean Sole	50M 10M prep.	161	Sole or roughy, banana, pineapple, orange juice
165	Salmon L'Orange	1Hr 10M prep.	147	Salmon fillets, Grand Marnier, orange juice
166	Tuna Oriental	20M	206	Tuna, almonds, green onion, peas
167	Broiled Scallops	35M 10M prep.	224	Scallops, white wine
168	Shrimp in Tomato Sauce	15M	192	Shrimp, tomato sauce, chili sauce
169	Sauteed Shrimp	15M	228	Shrimp, green beans, soy sauce, low sodium

THE MENU GUIDE
(Continued)

RED MEATS

Page	Recipes	Time	Calories	"Extra Ingredient Needs"
173	Stir-fried Beef	20M	158	Sirloin, mushrooms, green pepper, almonds, ginger
174	Oriental Stir-fry	20M 6Hr Marinade	156	Sirloin, orange juice, green pepper, onion
175	Sukiyaki	20M	372	Sirloin, tofu, waterchestnuts, oriental noodles, shiitake or regular mushrooms
176	Marinated Roast Beef	2Hr 4Hr marinade, 15M prep.	172	Rump or chuck roast, red wine, orange juice
177	Quick Roast Beef	1Hr 5M prep.	138	Sirloin or eye of round, beef boullion, mushroom
178	Meatloaf for the 90's	1 1/4Hr 25M prep.	340	Ground turkey, extra lean ground beef, celery, carrots, potatoes, yogurt, chili sauce
179	Chili	1 1/2Hr 30M prep.	95	Ground turkey or extra lean ground beef, kidney beans, tomato sauce, celery, chili powder
180	Shepherd's Pie	1Hr 30M prep.	315	Extra lean ground beef, carrots, peas, corn
181	Veal Lemon	20M	167	Veal cutlets, white wine, almonds, mozzarella
182	Veal Crescents in Wine Sauce	35M 20M prep.	189	Veal cutlets, spinach, chicken boullion, white wine
183	Lamb L'Orange	1Hr 15M prep.	302	Lamb leg or chops, orange juice, oranges
184	Pork Stir-fry	15M	171	Lean pork loin, pineapple

THE MENU GUIDE
(Continued)

DESSERTS

Page	Recipes	Time	Calories	"Extra Ingredient Needs"
187	Elegant Fruit Dessert	15M	169	Honey, strawberries, blueberries, peaches, kiwi
188	Souffle Almondine	45M 20M prep.	139	Milk, almond extract, eggs, almonds, strawberries
189	Frozen Chocolate Mousse	30M 2Hr Chill	166	Brandy, cocoa, chocolate chips, eggs, coffee, margarine, lowfat
190	Apricot Mousse	1Hr 30M prep.	153	Dried apricots, dry milk, eggs
191	Peach Tapioca	45M 15M ptrep.	77	Quick tapioca, milk, peaches
192	Chocolate Raspberry Brownies	45M	43	Almond extract, raspberries, cocoa, eggs low fat margarine, flour

COOKIES, CAKES & PIES

Page	Recipes	Time	Calories	"Extra Ingredient Needs"
195	Peanut Butter Cookies	40M	46	Peanut butter, eggs, sugar, Sweet'nLow
196	Buttery Sugar Cookies	30M	22	Lowfat margarine, eggs, half & half, flour
197	Linzer Cookies	35M	65	Almonds, raspberry jam, cookie recipe pg 196
198	Chocolate Chip Cookies	30M	34	Chocolate chips, egg substitute, brown sugar, eggs, lowfat margarine
199	Chocolate-Almond Cookies	40M 15M prep.	16	Eggs, almond extract, almonds, cocoa
200	"Ice Cream Icing"	15M	54	Lowfat margarine, canola oil, milk
201	Chocolate-Strawberry Torte	2Hr 35M prep.	209	Vanilla and plain yogurt, strawberries, cocoa, strawberry jam
202	Rich Chocolate Cake	1Hr 20M prep.	235	Milk, instant coffee, brandy, cocoa, sugar
203	Berry Cheesecake	1Hr 15M prep.	100	Recipe for yogurt cream cheese, oat bran graham crackers, strawberries or blueberries
204	Apple Spice Cake	11/2Hr	146	Lowfat margarine, plain yogurt, oat bran, apples

THE MENU GUIDE
(Continued)

COOKIES, CAKES & PIES (Continued)

Page	Recipe	Time	Calories	"Extra Ingredient Needs"
205	Pie Crust	20M	52	Oat bran, lowfat margarine, flour, salt
206	Apple Pie	11/2Hr 30M prep.	238	Apples, pie crust recipe
207	Peach-Blueberry Pie	11/2Hr 25M prep.	171	Peaches, blueberries, cornstarch, pie crust recipe
208	Strawberry-Rhubarb Pie	11/2Hr 25M prep.	164	Strawberries, rhubarb, pie crust recipe
209	Pumpkin Pie	11/2Hr 30M prep.	119	Canned pumpkin, evaporated skim milk, eggs, Brown Sugar Twin
210	Chocolate Pie	11/4Hr 45M prep.	181	Milk, dry milk, instant coffee, eggs, margarine

THE RECIPES

ABOUT THE RECIPES

Each recipe has been programmed on our computers. The nutritional information is listed for each recipe indicating the **calories, fat, carbohydrates, protein, cholesterol, sodium, iron, calcium, potassium and fiber.** per serving. Remember - if you have *second helpings* your intake doubles. The key to eating well and eating healthy is *moderation*.

"You can have your cake and eat it, too - just don't eat the whole cake!"

BREAKFASTS AND BREADS

Quick Carbohydrate Breakfast

Serves 2
10 Minutes

This energy-builder is even easier if you have an apple-slicer that cores and slices the apple for you.

2	tablespoons oats	2	tablespoons vanilla yogurt
2	tablespoons wheat germ	1	teaspoon cinnamon
2	tablespoons raisens	2/3	cup skim milk
2/3	cup apple, sliced		

Slice the apples and mix all the ingredients together. Enjoy this by itself or with juice and toast.

Nutrition information per serving: Calories: 140

Complex carbohydrates:	66%	Fat:	10%
Protein:	20%	Saturated fat:	3%
Iron:	2 mg	Monounsaturated fat:	2%
Calcium:	152 mg	Polyunsaturated fat:	4%
Potassium:	380 mg	Cholesterol:	2 mg
Fiber:	3 gm	Sodium:	57 mg

Breakfast Casserole

Serves 3
35 Minutes
(15 M preparation)

If you have a hungry family in the morning, make this up the night before and bake in the morning. It's nutritious, filling and easy to make with minimal clean-up. You may want to try adding a small amount of extra lean ham slices for a special taste.

4	slices wheat bread	1/2	teaspoon marjoram	
4	slices (2 ounces) monterey jack cheese, low-fat	Dash of pepper		
		1	teaspoon chives	
1	cup egg substitute	1/2	cup tomatoes, sliced or chopped	
2	egg whites	1	tablespoon parmesan cheese	
1	tablespoon onion, finely chopped (optional)			

Spray a small non-stick loaf pan with cooking spray. Lay 2 slices of bread on the bottom. Top with 2 slices of cheese and 1/4 cup of the tomatoes. Beat the egg substitute with the egg whites, onion and seasoning and pour one half of this over the cheese and tomatoes. Repeat the layers of bread, cheese, tomatoes and egg mixture again.

Top with parmesan cheese. Bake at 350 degrees for 20 minutes. Try topping each serving with apples and cinnamon. Serve with fresh fruit or juice for a complete breakfast.

Nutritional information per serving: Calories: 132

Complex carbohydrates:	32%	Fat:	29%
Protein:	31%	Saturated fat:	13%
Iron:	2 mg	Monounsaturated fat:	8%
Calcium:	115 mg	Polyunsaturated fat:	9%
Potassium:	250 mg	Cholesterol:	115 mg
Fiber:	3 gm	Sodium:	254 mg

Vegetable Omelet

Serves 4
20 Minutes

This is a healthy, filling way to start the day. Add whatever favorite vegetables you like.

1	tablespoon onion, chopped	3	tablespoons parsley
1/2	cup mushrooms, sliced	2	teaspoons chives
1/2	cup spinach, fresh or frozen	1	teaspoon basil
1/2	teaspoon sherry	Dash of pepper	
1/4	teaspoon soy sauce, low sodium	1/4	cup tomatoes, chopped
3/4	cup egg substitute	1/4	cup (1 ounce) monterey jack
2	egg whites		cheese, low-fat, shredded

Saute the onion, mushrooms and spinach in the sherry and soy sauce in a non-stick skillet until tender, then set aside. Beat the egg substitute and egg whites with the seasonings.

Pour the egg mixture into a hot non-stick skillet. When the mixture has set, sprinkle with the cheese and top with the vegetable mix and tomatoes. Fold over. Cook 1-2 minutes more until done.

Serve topped with plain yogurt and/or hot sauce.

Nutrition information per serving: Calories: 150

Complex Carbohydrates:	26%	Fat:	25%
Protein:	45%	Saturated fat:	10%
Iron:	3 mg	Monounsaturated fat:	14%
Calcium:	228 mg	Polyunsaturated fat:	1%
Potassium:	555 mg	Cholesterol:	13 mg
Fiber:	1 gm	Sodium:	304 mg

Apple-Cinnamon Bread Pudding

Serves 4
1 Hour
(20 M Preparation)

Make this up for a breakfast, brunch, lunch or snack.

2	slices wheat bread, cubed	1/2	teaspoon cinnamon
1	cup skim milk	1/2	teaspoon vanilla extract
1/2	cup egg substitute	1/4	teaspoon nutmeg
2	teaspoons sugar	11/4	cup apples, sliced
3	tablespoons Butter Buds	1	teaspoon brown sugar
3	tablespoons hot water		

Spread the bread cubes out on a cookie sheet and bake at 300 degrees for 5 minutes. Beat the milk. egg substitute and sugar together. In a separate bowl, mix the Butter Buds with the hot water to make a liquid butter.

Using a whisk, add 2 tablespoons of the liquid butter, cinnamon, extract and nutmeg beating well. Add the bread cubes.

Pour into a non-stick 9" or 10" square pan. Spread the apple slices over the bread cube mixture. Pour the remaining liquid butter over the apples and sprinkle with brown sugar. Bake at 300 degrees for 35-40 minutes.

Nutrition information per serving: Calories: 95

Complex carbohydrates:	53%	Fat:	7%
Protein:	25%	Saturated fat:	2%
Iron:	1 mg	Monounsaturated fat:	2%
Calcium:	93 mg	Polyunsaturated fat:	2%
Potassium:	219 mg	Cholesterol:	1 mg
Fiber:	2 gm	Sodium:	186 mg

French Toast

Serves 4 (2 slices each)
15 Minutes

French toast is so good on a cold morning. It's a great breakfast that's high in fiber. Try this recipe with yogurt and fruit or pourable fruit.

8	slices wheat bread	1	egg white
2	tablespoons Butter Buds	1	teaspoon white grape juice
1	teaspoon cinnamon	1	cup plain yogurt, non-fat
1/4	cup egg substitute	1	strawberries or blueberries

Pre-heat a non-stick skillet coated with cooking spray over medium-high heat.

Mix the Butter Buds, cinnamon, egg substitute, egg white and grape juice together. Dip each slice of bread in this batter and brown in the skillet on each side. Serve topped with yogurt and fruit.

Nutrition information per serving: Calories: 186

Complex carbohydrates:	51%	Fat:	20%
Protein:	20%	Saturated fat:	4%
Iron:	2 mg	Monounsaturated fat:	4%
Calcium:	185 mg	Polyunsaturated fat:	12%
Potassium:	375 mg	Cholesterol:	1mg
Fiber:	7 gm	Sodium:	334 mg

Pancakes

Serves 4 (2 pancakes each)
15 Minutes

These pancakes are pleasantly light and taste great. As with the French Toast, try them with the yogurt and fruit or a low-calorie pourable fruit syrup.

1/2	cup flour	1/2	teaspoon cinnamon
1/4	cup wheat flour	1/4	cup skim milk
1/2	teaspoon baking powder	2	tablespoons Butter Buds
1/3	cup white grape juice	2	tablespoons hot water
1/2	cup egg substitute	1/2	cup plain yogurt, non-fat
1	cup strawberries of blueberries, fresh or frozen		

Pre-heat a large skillet coated with cooking spray over medium-high heat.

Mix the flours, baking powder, grape juice, egg substitute, cinnamon and milk together. Spoon into the skillet to form 5" circles. When bubbles start to burst, turn and cook on other side (about 1-2 minutes each side).

Mix the Butter Buds with hot water to make a liquid butter. Serve the pancakes drizzled with the liquid butter, topped with yogurt and fruit.

Nutrition information per serving: Calories: 134

Complex carbohydrates:	76%	Fat:	2%
Protein:	21%	Saturated fat;	1%
Iron:	2 mg	Monounsaturated fat:	0%
Calcium:	132 mg	Polyunsaturated fat:	1%
Potassium:	354 mg	Cholesterol:	1 mg
Fiber:	2 gm	Sodium:	110 mg

Wheat Biscuits

Makes 24
40 Minutes
(30 M Preparation)

Did you think you would have to give up biscuits? Try these and you will have taste and good nutrition.

1	cup flour	2	teaspoons honey
1	cup wheat flour	1/4	cup margarine, low fat
2	teaspoons baking powder	1/2	cup plain yogurt, non-fat
1/2	teaspoon baking soda	1/2	cup skim milk or buttermilk
Dash salt		2	tablespoons skim milk

Sift the flours, baking powder, baking soda and salt together. In a separate bowl, mix the honey, margarine, yogurt and milk (preferably buttermilk). Gradually add the flour mixture.

Turn onto a flour surface and knead for 5 minutes. Then roll out to 1" thickness. Cut with a round cookie cutter.

Place the biscuits on a non-stick cookie sheet coated with cooking spray. Brush with milk. Bake at 400 degrees for 12-15 minutes.

Nutrition information per biscuit: Calories: 47

Complex carbohydrates:	65%	Fat:	20%
Protein:	14%	Saturated fat:	4%
Iron:	0 mg	Monounsaturated fat:	6%
Calcium:	45 mg	Polyunsaturated fat:	11%
Potassium:	124 mg	Cholesterol:	0 mg
Fiber:	1 gm	Sodium:	34 mg

"Indiana Scones"

Makes 16
45 Minutes
(25 M Preparation)

"Indiana Scones" are an adventure in bread. They are rich yet light. Slice and toast them for breakfast, dinner or snacking.

1	cup buttermilk	1	teaspoon baking soda
1	egg white	1/2	teaspoon salt
1/4	cup egg substitute	1/4	cup Butter Buds
1/2	teaspoon Sweet 'n Low	1/4	cup hot water
31/4	cups flour	2	tablespoons margarine
2	teaspoon baking powder	2	tablespoons skim milk

Mix the buttermilk, egg white, egg substitute and Sweet 'n Low together. In a separate bowl, Sift the flour, baking powder, baking soda and salt together. Mix the Butter Buds with the hot water and margarine.

Add 1/2 of the flour mixture to the buttermilk mixture, then the butter mixture. Add the remaining flour. Turn onto a floured surface and knead for 5 minutes. Separate the dough into 4 equal parts. Shape each into a ball, flatten to a thick circle 5 inches in diameter.

Cut the circles into quarters and place the triangles on a cookie sheet sprayed with cooking spray. Brush with milk. Bake at 400 degrees for 20 minutes.

Nutrition information per scone:

Calories: 84

Complex carbohydrates:	75%	Fat:	10%
Protein:	12%	Saturated fat:	2%
Iron:	1 mg	Monounsaturated fat:	3%
Calcium:	38 mg	Polyunsaturated fat:	5%
Potassium:	111 mg	Cholesterol:	1 mg
Fiber:	0 gm	Sodium:	171 mg

Apricot Tea Ring

Serves 16 (Slices)
2 Hours
(30 M Preparation)

This tea ring makes a great substitute for coffee cake. Try the "Streusel Topping" over the top.

1	pkg yeast	21/2	cups dried apricots
1/4	cup warm water	2	tablespoons water
1	tablespoon sugar	1	tablespoon sugar
2	tablespoons margarine, low fat	1/2	teaspoon cinnamon
2	tablespoons Butter Buds	1	tablespoon lemon juice
2	tablespoons hot water	1/2	teaspoon Sweet 'n Low
1	teaspoon salt	1/8	teaspoon salt
3/4	cup skim milk, scalded	4	tablespoons plain yogurt, non-fat
1/4	cup egg substitute	4	tablespoons almonds, sliced
23/4	cups flour		

Soften the yeast in the water. In a separate bowl, mix the Butter Buds and hot water. Add the sugar, margarine, salt and milk. Cool. Add the egg subsitute and yeast. Gradually mix in the flour. Roll the dough onto a floured surface to form a 12x15 rectangle.

In a sauce pan, mix the apricots, water, sugar, cinnamon, lemon juice, Sweet 'n Low and salt together. Heat over medium low heat until thick.

Spread the dough with yogurt and evenly spread the apricot mixture over the rectangle. Sprinkle with almonds. Roll the dough up like a jelly-roll starting with the wider side.

Place on a cookie sheet coated with cooking spray forming a ring with the dough. Cut 1" slices in the ring with scissors. Cover, let rise for 1 hour. Bake at 350 degrees for 25-30 minutes.

Nutrition information per slice:

Calories: 126

Complex carbohydrates:	74%	Fat:	10%
Protein:	9%	Saturated fat:	2%
Iron:	2 mg	Monounsaturated fat:	5%
Calcium:	61 mg	Polyunsaturated fat:	4%
Potassium:	414 mg	Cholesterol:	0 mg
Fiber:	2 gm	Sodium:	306 mg

81

Dinner Rolls

Makes 12 Rolls
3 1/2 Hours
(20 M Preparation)

These are delicious dinner rolls that are as low in calories as a slice of bread. The original of this recipe was 123 calories per roll; this version is almost half that.

1	package yeast	1	teaspoon salt
3	tablespoons lukewarm water	1/2	cup skim milk, scalded
1/2	teaspoon Sweet 'n Low	1/4	cup egg substitute
3	tablespoons Butter Buds	1	egg white
1	tablespoon margarine, low fat	21/4	cups flour

Soften the yeast in the warm water. Set aside. In a large bowl, combine the Sweet 'n Low, Butter Buds, margarine, salt and milk. Stir in the egg substitute, egg white and yeast. Gradually add the flour to the desired consistency.

Turn onto a floured surface and knead for 5 minutes. Place in a bowl coated with cooking spray. Cover and let rise in a warm place for 1 hour. Turn, and let rise, covered, for 1 hour more.

Shape into small balls and place each in muffin cups sprayed with cooking spray. Cover and let rise 45 minutes more. Bake at 400 degrees for 12 minutes.

Nutrition information per roll: Calories: 85

Complex carbohydrates:	80%	Fat:	2%
Protein:	17%	Saturated fat:	1%
Iron:	1 mg	Monounsaturated fat:	0%
Calcium:	52 mg	Polyunsaturated fat:	1%
Potassium:	157 mg	Cholesterol:	0 mg
Fiber:	1 gm	Sodium:	123 mg

Dinner Cheese Rolls

Makes 24 Rolls
2 1/4 Hour
(30 M Preparation)

These rolls have enough flavor, you may not need margarine on them!

1	pkg yeast	3	tablespoons plain yogurt, no-fat
1/2	cup warm water	1/2	cup monterey jack cheese
2	tablespoons Butter Buds		low fat, shredded
1	teaspoon hot water	1/2	cup cheddar cheese, low fat,
1	tablespoon sugar		shredded
1/2	teaspoon salt	1/4	cup egg substitute
1/2	teaspoon garlic	1	egg white, slightly beaten
1/4	cup skim milk	2	cups flour
1/2	teaspoon Sweet 'n Low	1	cup wheat flour
11/2	tablespoons margarine		

Combine the yeast and water. Set aside. Mix the Butter Buds with the hot water. Add the sugar, salt, garlic, milk, Sweet 'n Low, margarine and yogurt.

To the milk mixture, add the yeast, cheeses, egg substitute and egg white. Gradually add the flours. Knead on a floured surface for 5 minutes unitl smooth and elastic. Place the dough in a bowl coated with cooking spray, cover and let rise 1 hour.

Pinch 3" balls from the dough and place in each muffin cup coated with cooking spray. Cover and let rise 30 minutes. Bake at 425 degrees for 10-15 minutes.

Nutrition information per roll:

		Calories: 74	
Complex carbohydrates:	57%	Fat:	24%
Protein:	17%	Saturated fat:	10%
Iron:	1 mg	Monounsaturated fat:	8%
Calcium:	50 mg	Polyunsaturated fat:	6%
Potassium:	53 mg	Cholesterol:	4 mg
Fiber:	1 gm	Sodium:	97mg

Whole Wheat-Oatmeal Bread

Makes 36 slices (2 loaves)
4 Hours
(40 M Preparation)

This is a hearty bread that does take time for the yeast to rise, but the nutritional value is worth the wait.

1/4	cup Butter Buds	2	tablespoons yeast
1	tablespoon hot water	1/3	cup lukewarm water
1	cup skim milk	1/2	cup wheat germ
1	cup plain yogurt, non-fat	1	cup oats
2	teaspoons salt	5	cups whole wheat flour
3	tablespoons honey	1	egg white, lightly beaten
11/2	tablespoons margarine		

Mix the Butter Buds with hot water. Heat the milk over medium heat and add yogurt, butter liquid, salt, honey and margarine. Pour into a large bowl and let cool.

In a separate bowl, dissolve the yeast in the lukewarm water. Let it sit 2 minutes. Add the yeast to the milk mixture. Add the wheat germ, oats and half the flour. Stir well and add the remaining flour. (The dough will be very stiff) Turn the dough onto a floured surface and knead until it is smooth and elastic.

Place in a bowl coated with cooking spray, cover and let rise 1 hour. Punch it down and let rise 1 hour. Knead once again and shape into two loaves. Place each loaf in a non-stick loaf pan coated with cooking spray and let rise 45 minutes. Brush the tops with egg white. Bake the loaves at 375 degrees for 45 minutes. Turn the loaves out on racks to cool.

Nutrition information per slice:

Calories: 84

Complex carbohydrates:	69%	Fat:	7%
Protein:	18%	Saturated fat:	1%
Iron:	1 mg	Monounsaturated fat:	2%
Calcium:	26 mg	Polyunsaturated fat:	4%
Potassium:	199 mg	Cholesterol:	0 mg
Fiber:	3 gm	Sodium:	107 mg

SAUCES, TOPPINGS, DIPS & DRESSINGS

Dijon Dressing

Serves 16 (2 tablespoons per serving)
15 Minutes

This is our favorite dressing. It has a tangy flavor that compliments any salad and can be used on sandwiches and over vegetables, too.

4	tablespoons vinegar, balsamic or raspberry	1/2	teaspoon garlic
1/2	cup onion, minced	4	tablespoons dijon mustard
Dash salt		1	tablespoon basil
Dash pepper		2	teaspoons lemon juice
2	tablespoons water	1/4	cup canola oil
		1/4	cup sesame oil

Combine all ingredients in a food processor, gradually adding the oils last. Dressing can be stored refrigerated for up to 1 month.

Nutrition information per serving: Calories: 65

Complex carbohydrates:	34%	Fat:	93%
Protein:	0%	Saturated fat:	10%
Iron:	0 mg	Monounsaturated fat:	49%
Calcium:	3 mg	Polyunsaturated fat:	34%
Potassium:	29 mg	Cholesterol:	0 mg
Fiber:	0 gm	Sodium:	50 mg

Yogurt Dressing

Serves 8 (2 tablespoons per serving)
10 Minutes

This dressing makes a great substitute for the heavier dressings high in fat.

1/4	cup plain yogurt, non-fat	1/2	teaspoon basil
1	tablespoon skim milk	1/4	teaspoon oregano
1	teaspoon lemon juice	1/4	teaspoon chives
1/4	teaspoon horseradish	1/4	teaspoon honey
1	tablespoon onion, minced	2	teaspoons worchestershire sauce, low sodium

Combine all ingredients. Store in the refrigerator in an air-tight container. Serve on salads.

Nutrition information per serving: Calories: 9

Complex carbohydrates:	39%	Fat:	2%
Protein:	27%	Saturated fat:	1%
Iron:	0 mg	Monounsaturated fat:	0%
Calcium:	21 mg	Polyunsaturated fat:	1%
Potassium:	31 mg	Cholesterol:	0 mg
Fiber:	1 gm	Sodium:	18 mg

Creamy Coleslaw

Serves 4 (3/4 cup servings)
5 Minutes

Cabbage is one of the healthiest foods you can eat. Use this recipe to make coleslaw with less fat than traditional dressings.

21/2 cups shredded cabbage	1/2 teaspoon dry mustard <u>or</u>
1/3 cup buttermilk	regular mustard
11/2 tablespoon lite mayonnaise	1/2 teaspoon vinegar
1/2 cup plain yogurt, non-fat	1/4 teaspoon horseradish (or to taste)
1 teaspoon celery seeds	Dash salt & pepper

Combine all ingredients and store in the refrigerator in an air-tight container. Serve as your salad.

Nutrition information per serving: Calories: 55

Complex carbohydrates:	46%	Fat:	28%
Protein:	23%	Saturated fat:	8%
Iron:	0 mg	Monounsturated fat:	8%
Calcium:	116 mg	Polyunsaturated fat:	12%
Potassium:	287 mg	Cholesterol:	3 mg
Fiber:	1 gm	Sodium:	134 mg

A Dip for All Reasons

Serves 6 (2 tablespoons per serving)
5 Minutes

Use this dip as a topping for baked potatoes, a dip for raw vegetables or whatever you prefer.

1/2	cup plain yogurt, non-fat	1/4	teaspoon vanilla extract
1/4	teaspoon paprika	1/2	teaspoon basil
1	teaspoon onion, minced	Dash pepper	
1	tablespoon chives	Dash worchestershire sauce, low sodium	
1/2	tablespoon parsley		

Combine all ingredients and serve chilled.

Nutrition information per serving: Calories: 19

Complex carbohydrates:	53%	Fat:	1%
Protein:	41%	Saturated fat:	1%
Iron:	0 mg	Monounsaturated fat:	0%
Calcium:	65 mg	Polyunsaturated fat:	0%
Potassium:	90 mg	Cholesterol:	1 mg
Fiber:	0 gm	Sodium:	25 mg

Tuna Dip

Enjoy this recipe as an appetizer or as a tuna salad for lunch.

1/2	teaspoon lemon juice	1	tablespoon plain yogurt, non-fat
1/2	teaspoon chives	1	tablespoon light mayonnaise
8	ounces albacore tuna, packed in water, rinsed and drained	1/8	teaspoon worchestershire sauce, low sodium
1/2	teaspoon basil	2	teaspoons parmesan cheese,grated
1/8	teaspoon garlic		

Combine all ingredients, mixing well. Serve on bread or crackers or on a bed of lettuce.

Nutrition information per serving:

Calories: 52

Complex carbohydrates:	10%	Fat:	19%
Protein:	75%	Saturated fat:	6%
Iron:	0 mg	Monounsaturated fat:	4%
Calcium:	14 mg	Polyunsaturated fat:	10%
Potassium:	70 mg	Cholesterol:	15 mg
Fiber:	0 gm	Sodium:	48 mg

Salmon Dip

Serves 6 (3 tablespoons per serving)
10 Minutes

This Salmon Dip is richer tasting than the Tuna Dip. Try it as an appetizer on artichoke hearts on crackers.

1/2	teaspoon lemon juice	1	tablespoon plain yogurt, non-fat
1/2	teaspoon chives	1	tablespoon light mayonnaise
1/2	teaspoon basil	2	teaspoons parmesan cheese, grated
8	ounces canned salmon, packed in water, rinsed & drained	1/4	teaspoon garlic

Combine all ingredients. (If you prefer, mash the salmon bones with the salmon. This provides extra calcium.) Store in the refrigerator.

Nutrition information per serving: Calories: 56

Complex carbohydrates:	4%	Fat:	34%
Protein:	60%	Saturated fat:	9%
Iron:	0 mg	Monounsaturated fat:	10%
Calcium:	18 mg	Polyunsaturated fat:	15%
Potassium:	136 mg	Cholesterol:	21 mg
Fiber:	0 gm	Sodium:	51 mg

Cheese Sauce

Serves 8 (3 tablespoons per serving)
10 Minutes

The original recipe for this came from Cumberland Packing Corp., makers of Butter Buds.

11/2	tablespoons flour	1/2	teaspoon worchestershire sauce, low sodium
1	cup skim milk		
2	tablespoons Butter Buds	1/2	cup monterey jack cheese, low fat, shredded

Over low heat, combine the flour and milk stirring with a whisk. Add the Butter Buds, worchestershire sauce and cheese. Continue stirring until cheese is melted and the sauce is smooth and creamy.

Nutrition information per serving: Calories: 46

Complex carbohydrates:	26%	Fat:	34%
Protein:	38%	Saturated fat:	23%
Iron:	0 mg	Monounsturated fat:	9%
Calcium:	116 mg	Polyunsaturated fat:	1%
Potassium:	63 mg	Cholesterol:	7 mg
Fiber:	0 gm	Sodium:	94 mg

*Commercial product information per serving: Calories: 312

Complex carbohydrates:	10%	Fat:	68%
Protein:	20%	Saturated fat:	44%
Sodium:	337 mg	Cholesterol:	75 mg

Chocolate Sauce

Serves 6 (2 tablespoon servings)
10 Minutes

Did you think you could never have chocolate sauce without feeling guilty? Don't give up yet. This version tastes almost as good as the real thing with less saturated fat and calories.

3	tablespoons Butter Buds	1/2	teaspoon vanilla extract
2	tablespoons hot water	1	teaspoon canola oil
1/3	cup cocoa	1/2	teaspoon instant coffee
1	teaspoon sugar	3	tablespoons skim milk
11/2	teaspoon Sweet 'n Low	1	teaspoon non-fat dry milk

Mix the Butter Buds with the hot water. In a saucepan, combine the cocoa, sugar and sweetener. Add the Butter Buds, vanilla, oil and coffee. Cook over low heat. Add the milk and dry milk gradually, stirring with a whisk to smooth out lumps. Heat for 3-5 minutes, stirring constantly.

Nutrition information per serving: Calories: 44

Complex carbohydrates:	39%	Fat:	33%
Protein:	19%	Saturated fat:	11%
Iron:	1 mg	Monounsaturated fat:	16%
Calcium:	33 mg	Polyunsaturated fat:	5%
Potassium:	143 mg	Cholesterol:	1 mg
Fiber:	2 mg	Sodium:	56 mg

*Original recipe nutrition per serving: Calories: 50

Complex carbohydrates:	4%	Fat:	36%
Protein:	4%	Saturated fat:	23%

Streusel Topping

Sprinkle this topping over fruit or fruit pies instead of using whipped cream.

1/3	cup flour	1	tablespoon canola oil
1	teaspoon cinnamon	3	tablespoons brown sugar
1	teaspoon cocoa		

Mix the flour, cinnamon and cocoa, blending well. Gradually stir in the oil and brown sugar.
Mixture should be crumbly.

Nutrition information per serving:

Calories: 40

Complex carbohydrates:	26%	Fat:	41%
Protein:	6%	Saturated fat:	5%
Iron:	0 mg	Monounsaturated fat:	23%
Calcium:	14 mg	Polyunsaturated fat:	13%
Potassium:	30 mg	Cholesterol:	0 mg
Fiber:	0 gm	Sodium:	12 mg

Coffee Creamer

Makes 48 (1 teaspoon per serving)
5 Minutes

This is a coffee creamer that is less calories and less fat, but tastes as rich as the original creamers in your coffee.

1/4 **cup commercial dry coffee creamer**	3/4 **cup nonfat dry milk**

Combine both and store in an airtight conatiner.

Nutrition information per serving: Calories: 10

Complex carbohydrates:	50%	Fat:	16%
Protein:	33%	Saturated fat:	16%
Iron:	0 mg	Monounsaturated fat:	0 mg
Calcium:	24 mg	Polyunsaturated fat:	0 mg
Potassium:	38 mg	Cholesterol:	0 mg
Fiber:	0 gm	Sodium:	11 mg

*Original recipe information per serving: Calories: 11

Complex carbohydrates:	36%	Fat:	62%
Protein:	9%	Saturated fat:	62%

Yogurt Cream Cheese

Serves 8 (2 tablespoons per serving)
6-8 Hours
(5 M Preparation)

This method allows you to have cream cheese on bagels, in cheesecakes, anyway you like it, without the exceptionally high fat of regular cream cheese.

1	32 ounce carton of Dannon plain yogurt, non-fat
1	10" square piece of cheesecloth

Spoon the yogurt into the cheesecloth and set over a bowl to drain. (Cut a hole in lid of the carton and set the yogurt bag on top to drain.) Drain for 6-8 hours.

*For cream cheese for cheesecake, use low-fat vanilla yogurt instead.

Nutrition information per serving: Calories: 70

Complex carbohydrates:	54%	Fat:	2%
Protein:	44%	Saturated fat:	2%
Iron:	0 mg	Monounsaturated fat:	0%
Calcium:	251 mg	Polyunsaturated fat:	0%
Potassium:	321 mg	Cholesterol:	2 mg
Fiber:	0 gm	Sodium:	97 mg

*Original product information per serving: Calories: 100

Complex carbohydrates:	4%	Fat:	88%
Protein:	8%	Saturated fat:	58%

97

Whipped Topping

This whipped topping has a sweet, slightly tart flavor. Make it when you need it, as it will only keep for 1 day.

1	egg white	1/4	cup vanilla yogurt
1/4	teaspoon sugar		

Beat the egg white until stiff. Add the sugar and beat 1 minute more. Fold in the yogurt carefully.

Refrigerate in a covered container.

Nutrition information per serving: Calories: 14

Complex carbohydrates:	28%	Fat:	9%
Protein:	39%	Saturated fat:	6%
Iron:	0 mg	Monounsaturated fat:	2%
Calcium:	22 mg	Polyunsaturated fat:	1%
Potassium:	36 mg	Cholesterol:	1 mg
Fiber:	0 gm	Sodium:	18 mg

SOUPS & STEWS

Crab Bisque

Serves 10 (1/2 cup servings)
20 Minutes

This is our favorite soup. It is incredibly easy to make if you have a food processor. It's flavor appeals to nearly everyone.

20	ounces imitation crab	31/2	cup skim milk
1/2	cup onion, chopped	3	tablespoons parsley
2	tablespoons margarine, low fat	Dash salt	
1/4	cup flour	Dash pepper	
1/4	cup sherry	1/4	teaspoon hot sauce
1/2	cup mushrooms	1/8	teaspoon worchestershire sauce, low sodium
1/4	cup potatoes, shredded		
	1/4	teaspoon paprika	

Cut the crab into very small pieces, or coarsely chop in a food processor. Saute the onions in the margarine in a large non-stick pot. Add the flour, sherry and mushrooms, stirring until smooth.

Add the potatoes, milk, crab and parsley. Cook over low heat for 2 minutes. Season with salt, pepper, hot sauce and worchestershire sauce. Simmer 5 minutes more or longer.

Serve topped with paprika.

Nutrition information per serving: Calories: 115

Complex carbohydrates:	48%	Fat:	10%
Protein:	33%	Saturated fat:	2%
Iron:	1 mg	Monounsaturated fat:	3%
Calcium:	115 mg	Polyunsaturated fat:	5%
Potassium:	257 mg	Cholesterol:	6 mg
Fiber:	0 gm	Sodium:	369 mg

Gazpacho Soup

Serves 8 (3/4 cup servings)
35 Minutes

Make a big turrine of this. It's so good and it will keep at least a week. Try it with pasta salad.

3/4	cup tomatoes, chopped	1/4	teaspoon oregano
2	celery stalks	1	tablespoon basil
3/4	cup cucumber, peeled, chopped	1/2	teaspoon hot sauce
1/2	cup onion, chopped	Dash	pepper
2	garlic cloves, minced	Dash	salt
1/4	cup vinegar	1	tablespoon horseradish
2	tablespoons canola oil	6	cups canned tomatoes, low sodium
1	teaspoon worchestershire sauce, low sodium		

Chop all in a food processor or by hand and combine. Chill 1 hour or more.

Serve hot or cold.

Nutrition information per serving: Calories: 58

Complex carbohydrates:	60%	Fat:	26%
Protein:	13%	Saturated fat:	2%
Iron:	1 mg	Monounsaturated fat:	15%
Calcium:	50 mg	Polyunsaturated fat:	8%
Potassium:	490 mg	Cholesterol:	0 mg
Fiber:	4 gm	Sodium:	28 mg

Vichyssoise

Serves 4 (3/4 cup servings)
50 Minutes
(20M Preparation)

Served hot or cold, this soup has a rich, buttery flavor. This version is high in complex carbohydrates and low in fat. Make extra and have it for lunch, dinner or after-work snacking.

1/4	teaspoon margarine, low fat		2	packets chicken boullion, low sodium
3	green onions, chopped		2	cups water
1/2	cup onion, chopped		1/2	cup skim milk
1	celery stalk, sliced		1/3	cup plain yogurt, non fat
2	tablespoons Butter Buds		Dash	pepper
13/4	cup potatoes, diced		2	teaspoons chives
1/2	teaspoon basil		2	slices bacon, low salt, very well done

Saute the onions and celery in the margarine in a large non-stick pan. Add the Butter Buds, potatoes and basil. Mix the boullion and water and add to the mixture. Bring to a boil and then simmer, covered, for 15 minutes.

Pour into a food processor or blender and puree for 5 seconds. Pour the soup back into the pan over heat. Add the milk, yogurt and pepper. Cook 20 minutes more over low heat.

Serve topped with chives and crumbled bacon.

Nutrition information per serving:

Calories: 148

Complex carbohydrates:	72%	Fat:	10%
Protein:	14%	Saturated fat:	4%
Iron:	0 mg	Monounsaturated fat:	4%
Calcium:	94 mg	Polyunsaturated fat:	2%
Potassium:	811 mg	Cholesterol:	4 mg
Fiber:	2 gm	Sodium:	152 mg

Creamy Mushroom Soup

Serves 4 (1 cup servings)
45 Minutes
(20 M Preparation)

This soup makes a good base for other soups. It is a delicious soup that compliments any dinner.

4	packets chicken boullion, low sodium	2	cups mushrooms, sliced
4	cups water	1/2	cup mushrooms, pureed
1	cup potatoes, shredded	11/2	tablespoon flour
1/2	cup onion, chopped	1/4	cup water
1/2	cup carrot, sliced	1	tablespoon sherry
1	teaspoon basil	1/4	cup mozzarella cheese, low fat, shredded
1/2	teaspoon marjoram	1	tablespoon parsley
Dash pepper			

Mix the boullion and water and bring to a boil in a large pot. Add the potato, stir well and simmer 15 minutes.

Pour into a blender and puree. Pour back into the pot and add the basil, marjoram, pepper, mushrooms and flour. Add the sherry and cook 15 minutes more.

Serve topped with cheese and parsley.

Nutrition information per serving: Calories: 93

Complex carbohydrates:	64%	Fat:	6%
Protein:	18%	Saturated fat:	4%
Iron:	1 mg	Monounsaturated fat:	2%
Calcium:	45 mg	Polyunsaturated fat:	1%
Potassium:	1247 mg	Cholesterol:	4 mg
Fiber:	2 gm	Sodium:	35 mg

Hearty Meat & Pasta Soup

Serves 6 (11/2 cup servings)
45 Minutes
(15 M Preparation)

This recipe was created from a soup I had tried in a fine restaurant. It was truly unique and so good that it had to be tried at home.

6	ounces turkey sausage <u>or</u> extra lean ground beef	12	cups water
1	cup celery , sliced	1/3	cup red wine
1	cup carrots, sliced	3/4	cup fettucini, broken in pieces
1	cup onions, chopped	1/2	cup mushrooms
1	garlic clove, minced	11/2	tablespoons basil
Dash	pepper	10	ounces spinach, frozen, thawed
1/4	teaspoon worchestershire sauce, low sodium	2	tablespoons parmesan cheese

Saute the meat, celery, carrots, onions, garlic, pepper and worchestershire sauce in a non-stick skillet. Put the water in a large pot and add the meat and vegetables. Simmer for 15 minutes.

Stir in the wine, fettucini, mushrooms, basil and spinach. Simmer for 15 minutes or longer. Serve topped with parmesan.

Nutrition information per serving:

Calories: 110

Complex carbohydrates:	45%	Fat:	22%
Protein:	26%	Saturated fat:	10%
Iron:	2 mg	Monounsaturated fat:	9%
Calcium:	133 mg	Polyunsaturated fat:	3%
Potassium:	383 mg	Cholesterol:	25 mg
Fiber:	3 gm	Sodium:	121 mg

Corn Chowder

Serves 8 (1 cup servings)
11/4 Hour
(20 M Preparation)

This soup makes a great lunch or serve a small cup before dinner on a cold day. It's nutritional value is extremely good.

1	teaspoon canola oil	2	slices bacon, low-salt, very well done
1/2	cup onion, chopped	4	cups water
1/2	cup celery, sliced	2	tablespoons Butter Buds
1	cup carrots, peeled, sliced	Dash salt	
1	cup potatoes, finely chopped	Dash pepper	
1	cup corn, frozen	11/4	cup skim milk
1/4	teaspoon rosemary	2	tablespoons flour
1/2	teaspoon basil	1	teaspoon paprika
1	teaspoon chives	2	tablespoon parsley
1	tablespoon worchestershire sauce, low sodium		

In a large pot, saute the onion, celery, carrots in the oil 5 minutes. Add the potatoes, corn, basil, chives, worchestershire sauce and bacon. Cook 2 minutes more.

Add the water, Butter Buds, salt and pepper. Mix the flour with a small amount of the milk. Then add the flour and all the milk to the soup.

Bring to a boil, then cover and simmer 45 minutes or more. Serve topped with paprika and parsley.

Nutrition information per serving: Calories: 125

Complex carbohydrates:	80%	Fat:	6%
Protein:	12%	Saturated fat:	2%
Iron:	7 mg	Monounsaturated fat:	3%
Potassium:	373 mg	Polyunsaturated fat:	1%
Calcium:	67 mg	Cholesterol:	2 mg
Fiber:	5 gm	Sodium:	115 mg

Chicken Noodle Soup

Serves 8 (1/2 cup servings)
3 Hours
(25 M Preparation)

Chicken noodle soup is good not only when you're sick. This one is rich in complex carbohydrates.

1/2	cup onion, chopped	1	tablespoon basil
1	celery stalk, sliced	1	tablespoon parsley
2	carrots, sliced	1	teaspoon thyme
1/4	teaspoon margarine, low fat	2	tablespoons Butter Buds
1	pound chicken breasts, boneless	1	tablespoon flour
4	cups water	1/4	cup water
1/4	cup potato, shredded	6	ounces eggless noodles, cooked
Dash	pepper		

Saute the celery, carrots and onion in the margarine in a large pot. Remove the skin and fat from the chicken and cut into bite-size pieces. Add the chicken to the pot. Cook 2-3 minutes.

Add the water, potato, parsley, basil, thyme and Butter Buds. Simmer 2 hours. Add the noodles and simmer 30 minutes more.

Nutrition information per serving: Calories: 73

Complex carbohydrates:	52%	Fat:	10%
Protein:	36%	Saturated fat:	3%
Iron:	1 mg	Monounsaturated fat:	4%
Calcium:	17 mg	Polyunsaturated fat:	3%
Potassium:	145 mg	Cholesterol:	24 mg
Fiber:	1 gm	Sodium:	44 mg

Chicken Stew

Serves 8 (1 cup servings)
11/4 Hour
(25 M Preparation)

The combination of chicken and vegetables makes a hearty stew. It's as filling and tasty as a beef stew.

1	teaspoon canola oil	4	cups water
1/2	cup onion, chopped	1/4	cup white wine
1	pound chicken breasts, boneless	2	teaspoons worchestershire sauce, low sodium
2	carrots, sliced		
2	celery stalks, sliced	2	cups potatoes, diced
1/4	teaspoon garlic	2	cups green beans
Dash	salt	1	cup peas
Dash	pepper	1	cup mushrooms, sliced
1/4	cup flour	1	packet chicken boullion, low sodium
2	tablespoons Butter Buds	1/2	cup water
1	teaspoon basil	1	tablespoon parsley

In a large pot saute the onion in the oil. Remove the skin and fat from the chicken and cut into bite-size pieces. Add the chicken, carrots and celery to the onion along with the garlic, salt and pepper.

Add the flour, Butter Buds and basil and toss with the chicken mixture. Simmer covered for 15 minutes.

Add the water, wine, worchestershire sauce and potatoes and simmer 15 minutes more. Mix the boullion and water. Then add the peas, beans, mushrooms and broth. Simmer 30 minutes more.

Nutrition information per serving: Calories: 160

Complex carbohydrates:	50%	Fat:	10%
Protein:	35%	Saturated fat:	2%
Iron:	2 mg	Monounsaturated fat:	4%
Calcium:	45 mg	Polyunsaturated fat:	3%
Potassium:	556 mg	Cholesterol:	29 mg
Fiber:	4 gm	Sodium:	105 mg

VEGETABLES AND GRAINS

Stir-fried Vegetables

Serves 4
25 Minutes

When you can't decide on which vegetable to fix, make them all! Choose an assortment according to your personal tastes.

1	teaspoon canola oil	1/2	cup mushrooms, sliced
1/2	cup onion, chopped	1/2	cup pea pods
1/2	cup carrot, peeled, sliced	1/4	cup almonds. sliced
1/2	cup celery, sliced	1/2	teaspoon sesame oil
1/2	cup broccoli	1	tablespoon sesame seeds
1/2	cup bean sprouts		

You may use fresh or frozen vegetables. If you choose frozen, you will not need to thaw, just cook them as is!

Heat the oil in a non-stick skillet and saute the vegetables, starting with the carrots and celery. Cook over low heat until crisp-tender.

Add the almonds, oil and seeds. Cook another 2-3 minutes.

Nutrition information per serving: Calories: 78

Complex carbohydrates:	51%	Fat:	32%
Protein:	13%	Saturated fat:	5%
Iron:	1 mg	Monounsaturated fat:	17%
Calcium:	41 mg	Polyunsaturated fat:	11%
Potassium:	315 mg	Cholesterol:	0 mg
Fiber:	4 gm	Sodium:	33 mg

Corn on the Cob

Serves 4
15 Minutes
(5 M Preparation)

Preparing corn on the cob in the microwave is better tasting and the nutrients are not boiled out as in the old method.

4	ears of corn	Dash salt (optional)
1/4	cup Butter Buds	Dash pepper
1/4	cup hot water	

Husk the corn and place on a microwave-safe platter. Sprinkle with a little water and cover with a paper towel. Microwave on high for 10 minutes, turning at 5 minutes.

Mix the Butter Buds with the hot water.

Serve the corn with the liquid butter drizzled over and seasoned with salt and pepper. (Although the liquid butter has a slight salty taste and additional salt is not necessary.)

Nutrition information per serving: Calories: 91

Complex carbohydrates:	85%	Fat:	8%
Protein:	7%	Saturated fat:	1%
Iron:	1 mg	Monounsaturated fat:	2%
Calcium:	2 mg	Polyunsaturated fat:	4%
Potassium:	192 mg	Cholesterol:	0 mg
Fiber:	4 gm	Sodium:	132 mg

Vegetables in Cheese Sauce

Serves 4
15 Minutes

Make your vegetables special without adding the fat.

1/2 recipe "cheese sauce", pg 93	20	ounces fresh or frozen green beans, or broccoli or asparagus

If you are using fresh vegetables, steam for 15 minutes. If frozen, microwave until done.

Serve with cheese sauce over each serving.

Nutrition information per serving: Calories: 47

Complex carbohydrates:	65%	Fat:	1%
Protein:	34%	Saturated fat:	1%
Iron:	1 mg	Monounsaturated fat:	0%
Calcium:	63 mg	Polyunsaturated fat:	0%
Potassium:	371 mg	Cholesterol:	0 mg
Fiber:	4 gm	Sodium:	25 mg

Sesame Broccoli

Serves 4
10 Minutes

This is an easy way to add flavor to broccoli or any green vegetable.

20	ounces broccoli, frozen	2	tablespoons soy sauce, low sodium
1/2	teaspoon sesame oil	1	teaspoon honey
2	tablespoons sesame seeds		

Microwave the broccoli until tender, 6-8 minutes.

In a non-stick skillet, saute the oil and seeds until light brown. Toss in the broccoli, soy sauce and honey. Cook 1 minute more.

Nutrition information per serving: Calories: 82

Complex carbohydrates:	40%	Fat:	30%
Protein:	23%	Saturated fat:	5%
Iron:	1 mg	Monounsaturated fat:	12%
Calcium:	66 mg	Polyunsaturated fat:	14%
Potassium:	397 mg	Cholesterol:	0 mg
Fiber:	4 gm	Sodium:	123 mg

114

Green Beans Almondine

A special way to prepare green beans that appeals to everyone.

2	10 ounce packages frozen green beans	1/4	teaspoon soy sauce, low sodium
1	cup onion, chopped	1	tablespoon white wine
3/4	cup mushrooms, chopped	1/2	teaspoon basil
11/2	tablespoon almonds, sliced	1	tablespoon Butter Buds
		Dash pepper	

Cook the beans in the microwave (if you have fresh green beans, steam for 15 minutes).

Saute the onion, mushrooms and almonds in the soy sauce and wine. Add the green beans and season with the basil. Cook 5 minutes more. Serve topped with Butter Buds and pepper.

Nutrition information per serving:

Calories: 83

Complex carbohydrates:	64%	Fat:	16%
Protein:	14%	Saturated fat:	2%
Iron:	2 mg	Monounsaturated fat:	11%
Calcium:	83 mg	Polyunsaturated fat:	4%
Potassium:	408 mg	Cholesterol:	0 mg
Fiber:	4 gm	Sodium:	37 mg

Green Beans & Rice

Serves 4
25 Minutes
(5 M Preparation)

When your time and energy are short, this is a convenient way to make your vegetable and rice in one dish. Select a quick meat dish and you have a 30 minute dinner!

2/3	cup rice	1	cup green beans
1	tablespoon parsley	2	packets beef boullion, low sodium
1/3	cup onion	2	tablespoon monterey jack cheese, low fat
1/4	teaspoon marjoram		
1	cup skim milk	1/8	teaspoon salt
1/4	teaspoon garlic	1	tablespoon parmesan cheese

If you are using frozen green beans, thaw in the microwave. Then combine all ingredients (except the parmesan) in a casserole dish.

Top with parmesan cheese. Bake at 350 degrees for 20 minutes.

Nutrition information per serving: Calories: 112

Complex carbohydrates:	46%	Fat:	23%
Protein:	25%	Saturated fat:	15%
Iron:	1 mg	Monounsaturated fat:	7%
Calcium:	191 mg	Polyunsaturated fat:	1%
Potassium:	531 mg	Cholesterol:	10 mg
Fiber:	2 gm	Sodium:	175 mg

Summer Squash Cakes

Serves 4 (2 cakes per serving)
15 minutes

These have an incredibly good "buttery" taste - somewhat like corn fritters. They are best as a compliment to chicken or fish.

2	medium summer squash	1/4	cup flour
1/2	cup onion, finely chopped	11/2	teaspoon canola oil
1/2	cup egg substitute	1	tablespoon parmesan cheese
1/3	cup green pepper, chopped (optional)		Dash soy sauce

Grate the squash and squeeze dry. Combine with onion, egg substitute, green pepper and flour. Heat the oil in a non-stick skillet.

Drop the mixture by spoonfuls into the skillet and fry 2-3 minutes on each side until brown, turning carefully. Season lightly with soy sauce.

Serve topped with the parmesan cheese.

Nutrition information per serving: Calories: 68

Complex carbohydrates:	50%	Fat:	27%
Protein:	21%	Saturated fat:	6%
Iron:	1 mg	Monounsaturated fat:	18%
Calcium:	47 mg	Polyunsaturated fat:	3%
Potassium:	168 mg	Cholesterol:	1 mg
Fiber:	1 gm	Sodium:	53 mg

Spinach Souffle

Serves 4
25 Minutes
(10 M Preparation)

This is a special way to prepare spinach that helps dress up "ordinary" vegetables.

10	ounces frozen spinach	1	egg white, lightly beaten
1/4	teaspoon olive oil	1	tablespoon romano cheese
1/2	cup onion, chopped	Dash	salt
1/4	teaspoon garlic	Dash	pepper
1/4	teaspoon basil	2	teaspoons parmesan cheese, grated
1/2	cup egg substitute	1	tablespoon Butter Buds

Cook the spinach in the microwave. Saute the onion and garlic in the oil in a non-stick skillet.

To the spinach, beat in the basil, egg substitute, egg white and romano cheese, seasoning with salt and pepper. Stir in the onion mixture.

Pour the spinach mixture into a baking dish and top with Butter Buds and parmesan. Bake at 375 degrees for 10-15 minutes.

Nutrition information per serving: Calories: 67

Complex carbohydrates:	67%	Fat:	155%
Protein:	39%	Saturated fat:	6%
Iron:	2 mg	Monounsaturated fat:	6%
Calcium:	179 mg	Polyunsaturated fat:	3%
Potassium:	374 mg	Cholesterol:	2 mg
Fiber:	4 gm	Sodium:	187 mg

Spinach Quiche

Serves 6
1 Hour
(25 M preparation)

This recipe may take a little longer, but the preparation time is short and the result is a one-dish meal.

3/4	cup cheddar cheese, low fat shredded	1/2	cup skim milk
3/4	cup unbleached flour	2	tablespoons dry milk, nonfat
1/4	cup oat bran	2	tablespoons half & half
1	tablespoon canola oil	1/4	cup onion, chopped
1/4	cup Butter Buds	1/2	teaspoon nutmeg
1/4	cup hot water	1/2	teaspoon basil
Dash	salt	1/4	teaspoon marjoram
1/2	package frozen spinach (5 ounces), cooked	1/4	cup egg substitute
		1	egg white

Mix the 1/2 cup of the cheese, all the flour, oat bran and oil together. Mix the Butter Buds and hot water together. Add the liquid butter and salt to the cheese mixture. Press this into a quiche pan (or cake pan) coated with cooking spray.

Cook the spinach and dry thoroughly. Over low heat, combine the spinach, milk, dry milk, half & half, onion, seasoning, remaining cheese and seasoning. Heat until smooth.

Add the egg substitute and egg white. Pour into the quiche shell. Bake at 400 degrees for 15 minutes. Then lower oven to 350 degrees and bake for 20 minutes.

Nutrition information per serving: Calories: 255

Complex carbohydrates:	43%	Fat:	30%
Protein:	24%	Saturated fat:	11%
Iron:	2 mg	Monounsaturated fat:	13%
Calcium:	341 mg	Polyunsaturated fat:	7%
Potassium:	422 mg	Cholesterol:	18 mg
Fiber:	5 gm	Sodium:	471 mg

Special Spinach

The addition of well done, crispy bacon compliments the spinach, while maintaining good nutritional values.

2	10 ounce packages frozen spinach	3/4	cup warm water
1	cup onion, chopped	1	tablespoon cornstarch
2	tablespoons lemon juice	1	tablespoon basil
1/4	cup chicken broth	1/2	cup mushrooms, chopped
2	tablespoons white wine	Dash	pepper
		1	slice bacon, low salt, very well done

Cook the spinach in the microwave 5 minutes. Set aside.

Saute the onion in the broth and wine. Mix the cornstarch with the water and add to the onions, stirring constantly until thick.

Add the spinach, basil, mushrooms, pepper and crumble the bacon over all. Cook 5 minutes more or until done.

Nutrition information per serving: Calories: 97

Complex carbohydrates:	50%	Fat:	9%
Protein:	23%	Saturated fat:	3%
Iron:	3 mg	Monounsaturated fat:	3%
Calcium:	241 mg	Polyunsaturated fat:	3%
Potassium:	1747 mg	Cholesterol:	3 mg
Fiber:	6 gm	Sodium:	176 mg

Tomatoes Provencale

10 Minutes

This recipe is so easy to make. It is similar to that served in fine restaurants.

4	firm medium tomatoes	3	tablespoons bread crumbs
1/2	teaspoon canola oil	2	tablespoons onion, minced
Dash pepper		1	tablespoon mozzarella cheese, low fat, shredded
1	teaspoon basil		
1/2	teaspoon oregano	1	tablespoon parmesan cheese

Cut the tomatoes in half. Brush the tops lightly with oil. Mix the crumbs with the pepper, basil, oregano and onion. Sprinkle over the tomatoes.

Broil 2-3 minutes. Sprinkle the tomatoes with the cheese and broil 1 minute more.

Nutrition information per serving: Calories: 43

Complex carbohydrates:	52%	Fat:	27%
Protein:	16%	Saturated fat:	9%
Iron:	1 mg	Monounsaturated fat:	12%
Calcium:	47 mg	Polyunsaturated fat:	5%
Potassium:	219 mg	Cholesterol:	2 mg
Fiber:	2 gm	Sodium:	48 mg

Vegetable-Cheese Pie

Serves 4
45 Minutes
(15 M Preparation)

This is easy and requires few dishes to prepare. It can be a one-dish lunch or a side dish with a light entree.

2	teaspoons white wine	1	tablespoon parsley
1/2	cup carrot, peeled, sliced	1	teaspoon garlic
1/2	cup onion, chopped	1/4	cup egg substitute
1/2	cup mushrooms, chopped	1/3	cup ricotta cheese
1/2	cup green beans, frozen, thawed	1/3	cup cottage cheese, lowfat
2	cups tomatoes, chopped	1	egg white
Dash	pepper	1	tablespoon mozzarella cheese, lowfat, shredded
2	teaspoons basil		

Saute the vegetables in the wine and season with the pepper, basil, parsley and garlic until tender. Pour into a pie pan coated with cooking spray.

Combine the egg substitute, ricotta and cottage cheeses and egg white. Pour over the vegetables. Sprinkle the mozzarella on top and bake at 350 degrees for 30 minutes.

Nutrition information per serving: Calories: 109

Complex carbohydrates:	38%	Fat:	23%
Protein:	34%	Saturated fat:	14%
Iron:	1 mg	Monounsaturated fat:	6%
Calcium:	132 mg	Polyunsturated fat:	2%
Potassium:	408 mg	Cholesterol:	10 mg
Fiber:	3 gm	Sodium:	164 mg

Brown & Wild Rice

Serves 4
40 Minutes
(5 M Preparation)

Brown and wild rice are the most nutrient-dense rice. Try this recipe for ease and flavor.

1	cup brown rice	Dash soy sauce	
1/2	cup wild rice	1	packet chicken boullion, low
4	cups water		sodium

Combine the rice and water with the soy sauce and boullion in a microwave-safe baking dish. Cover microwave on high for 5 minutes.

Stir and microwave for 20 minutes more at medium. Stir, microwave for 15 minutes more at medium.

Nutrition information per serving: Calories: 78

Complex carbohydrates:	81%	Fat:	35
Protein:	12%	Saturated fat:	1%
Iron:	0 mg	Monounsaturated fat:	1%
Calcium:	8 mg	Polyunsaturated fat:	1%
Potassium:	342 mg	Cholesterol:	0 mg
Fiber:	0 gm	Sodium:	62 mg

Baked Potatoes Light

Serves 4
50 Minutes
(5 M Preparation)

Baked potatoes are an excellent source of good nutrition. What you put on them is important!

4	medium potatoes, 21/2" in diameter	1	tablespoon Butter Buds
		1	tablespoon chives
1	cup cottage cheese, low fat		Dash pepper

Make holes in the potatoes and bake in the oven at 375 degrees for 45 minutes (or microwave on high for 15-20 minutes, turning regularly).

Top each potato with the cottage cheese, Butter Buds, chives and pepper.

Nutrition information per serving:

Calories: 70

Complex carbohydrates:	48%	Fat:	7%
Protein:	45%	Saturated fat:	45
Iron:	0 mg	Monounsaturated fat:	2%
Calcium:	38 mg	Polyunsaturated fat:	1%
Potassium:	161 mg	Cholesterol:	3 mg
Fiber:	1 gm	Sodium:	231 mg

Fluffy Twice-Baked Potatoes

Serves 4
45 Minutes

These potatoes are light, yet filling. They have a wonderful flavor.

2	medium-large potatoes	3	tablespoons Butter Buds
3	tablespoons skim milk	2	tablespoons monterey jack cheese
1	tablspoon plain yogurt, non-fat	1	egg white
1	tablespoon chives	1	tablespoon cheddar cheese, lowfat
	Dash of salt	1/2	teaspoon paprika
	Dash of pepper		Parsley

Make holes with a fork at each end of the potatoes. Microwave at high for 10-15 minutes until done, turning frequently. Allow to cool.

Cut the potatoes in half lenghwise and scoop out the pulp, leaving a thin lining in the skins. Mash the pulp with the milk, yogurt, chives, salt, pepper, Butter Buds and monterey jack cheese. Beat the egg white until stiff and fold into the potato mixture.

Spoon the mixture into the skins and place them in a baking pan. Sprinkle the potatoes with cheddar cheese, paprika and parsley. Bake at 350 degrees for 15 minutes, until hot.

Nutrition information per serving: Calories: 98

Complex carbohydrates:	65%	Fat:	16%
Protein:	18%	Saturated fat:	10%
Iron:	0 mg	Monounsturated fat:	5%
Calcium:	87 mg	Polyunsaturated fat:	1%
Potassium:	268 mg	Cholesterol:	6 mg
Fiber:	1 gm	Sodium:	133 mg

125

Mashed Potatoes

Serves 4
20 Minutes
(10 M Preparation)

Even though you may not need a recipe for mashed potatoes, try this one to attain the flavor without adding excessive fat.

4	medium potatoes, 21/2" in diameter	1/4	cup skim milk
3	tablespoons Butter Buds	2	tablespoons plain yogurt, non-fat
		Dash pepper	

Peel the potatoes (although I prefer them unpeeled, it's better and easier) and cut into small pieces. Boil them in just enough water to cover for 10-15 minutes until tender.

Mash the potatoes with a mixer or hand masher, adding the Butter Buds, milk and yogurt, seasoning with pepper.

Nutrition information per serving: Calories: 129

Complex carbohydrates:	91%	Fat:	0%
Protein:	8%	Saturated fat:	0%
Iron:	0 mg	Monounsaturated fat:	0%
Calcium:	45 mg	Polyunsaturated fat:	0%
Potassium:	488 mg	Cholesterol:	1 mg
Fiber:	3 gm	Sodium:	63 mg

Creamed Potatoes and Peas

Serves 4
50 Minutes
(10 M Preparation)

Normally cream sauces are thought of as fattening. This one is not and yet provides a rich flavor.

3	medium potatoes, 2 1/2" in diameter	1/2	cup carrot, peeled, sliced
1	teaspoon canola oil	1/2	teaspoon cayenne pepper
Dash salt		1 1/2	cup water
1/2	teaspoon dry mustard	2	teaspoons cornstarch
1/2	cup onion, chopped	1	cup plain yogurt, non-fat
		2/3	cup frozen peas, thawed

Peel the potatoes and cut them into small pieces. Heat the oil in a non-stick skillet and saute the potatoes, onion and carrot, seasoning with salt and mustard. Cook for 10 minutes over medium heat.

Add the pepper and water, mixing the cornstarch with a small amount of water before adding to the mixture. Simmer over low heat for 30 minutes, stirring occasionally.

Add the yogurt and peas and simmer 5 minutes more.

Nutrition information per serving:

Calories: 160

Complex carbohydrates:	78%	Fat:	7%
Protein:	14%	Saturated fat:	1%
Iron:	1 mg	Monounsaturated fat:	1%
Calcium:	112 mg	Polyunsaturated fat:	5%
Potassium:	637 mg	Cholesterol:	1 mg
Fiber:	4 gm	Sodium:	161 mg

Gourmet Potatoes

Serves 4
45 Minutes
(20 M Preparation)

For an elegant dinner, these potatoes have great taste and a beautiful presentation. Serve this with a light meat entree.

3 1/2	cup potatoes, diced in cubes	1/4	cup monterey jack cheese, low fat
1/4	cup low salt chicken broth	1	onion, chopped
1	cup non-fat yogurt	2	tablespoons crushed almonds
1/2	cup mushrooms	1	tablespoon parmesan cheese

Boil the potatoes until tender, about 10 minutes. Combine the broth, yogurt, mushrooms, cheese and onion. Drain the potatoes and place in a baking dish coated with cooking spray. Pour the yogurt sauce over the potatoes.

Combine the almonds and parmesan and sprinkle over the sauce. Bake at 325 degrees for 25 minutes.

Nutrition information per serving: Calories 231

Complex carbohydrates:	61%	Fat:	14%
Protein:	19%	Saturated fat:	5%
Iron:	1 mg	Monounsaturated fat:	8%
Calcium:	221 mg	Polyunsaturated fat:	7%
Potassium:	1893 mg	Cholesterol:	8 mg
Fiber:	4 gm	Sodium:	127 mg

Crispy Fried Potatoes

Serves 4
20 Minutes

If you love home fries, but don't want all the fat that comes with frying, try this pan-fried method.

3	medium potatoes, unpeeled sliced very thin	3/4	cup onion, chopped
		1/2	cup green pepper (optional)
Dash pepper		1	teaspoon basil
1	teaspoon canola oil	1	tablespoon parmesan cheese, grated

Saute the potatoes in the oil in a non-stick skillet. Add the onion and green pepper and season with the pepper and basil to taste.

Brown until crisp, about 15-20 minutes. Serve topped with parmesan.

Nutrition information per serving: Calories: 127

Complex carbohydrates:	74%	Fat:	18%
Protein:	6%	Saturated fat:	4%
Iron:	1 mg	Monounsaturated fat:	12%
Calcium:	42 mg	Polyunsaturated fat:	2%
Potassium:	405 mg	Cholesterol:	1 mg
Fiber:	3 gm	Sodium:	30 mg

Stir-fried Rice

Serves 4
15 Minutes

This is an easy way to give rice more flavor without excessive sodium.

2	cups rice, cooked	11/2	teablespoon soy sauce, low sodium
3/4	cup mushrooms, sliced	1/2	teaspoon dark or light sesame oil
3/4	cup zucchini	1	tablespoon Butter Buds
1/4	cup chicken broth	1	tablespoon sesame seeds
3/4	cup onions, chopped	1/4	cup waterchestnuts or almonds (optional)

In a non-stick skillet saute the rice, mushrooms, zucchini and onions in the broth and soy sauce for 3-4 minutes.

Add the oil, Butter Buds, seeds and waterchestnuts. Saute 2 minutes more.

Nutrition information per serving: Calories: 164

Complex carbohydrates:	77%	Fat:	12%
Protein:	10%	Saturated fat:	2%
Iron:	1 mg	Monounsaturated fat:	4%
Calcium:	27 mg	Polyunsaturated fat:	5%
Potassium:	409 mg	Cholesterol:	0 mg
Fiber:	3 gm	Sodium:	175 mg

Barley with Vegetables

Serves 4
50 Minutes
(15 M Preparaton)

Barley is a nice change from potatoes and rice. This recipe gives the barley extra flavor.

1	teaspoon olive oil	1	tablespoon soy sauce, low sodium
1/2	teaspoon garlic	Dash pepper	
4	green onions, chopped	11/4	cup barley
3/4	cup mushrooms, chopped	4	cups water
10	ounces frozen green beans, french cut	Parsely	

In a large pan, saute the garlic, onions and mushrooms in the oil until tender.

Add the green beans, soy sauce, pepper, barley and water. Cover and simmer 30-40 minutes. Serve topped with parsley.

Nutrition information per serving: Calories: 89

Complex carbohydrates:	75%	Fat:	12%
Protein:	125	Saturated fat:	2%
Iron:	1 mg	Monounsaturated fat:	8%
Calcium:	37 mg	Polyunsturated fat:	25
Potassium:	251 mg	Cholesterol:	0 mg
Fiber:	3 gm	Sodium:	154 mg

PASTA

Pasta Salad

Serves 4
30 Minutes

Pasta salad is good for lunch or try it for dinner with a soup, for an easy meal. If you have last night's leftover chicken or steak, cut into bite size pieces and toss into the Pasta Salad.

4	tomatoes, chopped (2 cups)	11/2	tablespoons canola oil
1	cup onion, chopped		Dash of salt
1	teaspoon garlic		Dash of pepper
3	tabelspoons basil	6	ounces spiral pasta
2	teaspoons oregano	1	tablespoon parmesan cheese
2	tablespoons balsamic vinegar		

Combine the tomatoes, onion, garlic, basil, oregano, vinegar, oil, salt and pepper. Cover and refrigerate for 20 minutes. Cook the pasta. Toss the pasta with the vegetables and top with the parmesan. Serve hot or cold.

Nutrition information per serving: Calories: 240

Complex carbohydrates:	53%	Fat:	31%
Protein:	14%	Saturated fat:	6%
Iron:	4 mg	Monounsaturated fat:	13%
Calcium:	135 mg	Polyunsaturated fat:	13%
Potassium:	571 mg	Cholesterol:	71 mg
Fiber:	3 gm	Sodium:	109 mg

Spaghetti with Meat Sauce

Serves 6
50 Minutes
(15 M Preparation)

Spaghetti is filling and nutrtious. This recipe is easy and fairly quick.

1	teaspoon olive oil	1	8 ounce can tomato sauce, no salt
10	ounces extra lean ground beef	1	teaspoon oregano
		1	teaspoon basil
3/4	cup onion, chopped	2	tablespoons parsley
1	teaspoon garlic	Dash	salt and pepper
3/4	cup mushrooms, chopped	1	pound spaghetti pasta
1	6 ounce can tomato paste	3	tablespoons parmesan, ground
2	16 ounce cans whole tomatoes		

Heat the olive oil in a large, deep skillet. Brown the meat and onion, seasoning with the garlic. Add the mushrooms, tomato paste, tomatoes, tomato sauce, herbs and seasoning. Stir well and simmer over low heat for 30 minutes.

Cook the spaghetti pasta. Serve covered with sauce and topped with parmesan.

Nutrition information per serving: Calories: 256

Complex carbohydrates:	48%	Fat:	24%
Protein:	24%	Saturated fat:	9%
Iron:	5 mg	Monounsaturated fat:	12%
Calcium:	93 mg	Polyunsaturated fat:	3%
Potassium:	1184 mg	Cholesterol:	30 mg
Fiber:	6 gm	Sodium:	362 mg

New York Pasta

Serves 4
20 Minutes

This dish is a re-creation of a wonderful pasta I had in a little New York restaurant. It's taste is unique because it is rich, yet light. You may want to try romano in place of the parmesan.

1	recipe cheese sauce, pg. 93	1	tablespoon parsley
1	teaspoon olive oil	1/2	teaspoon oregano
3	cups tomatoes, chopped	1/4	teaspoon pepper
1	cup onion, chopped	1/2	teaspoon garlic
11/2	cups mushrooms, chopped	2	tablespoons basil
8	ounces angel hair pasta	1	tablespoons parmesan cheese

Make the cheese sauce. Keep warm over low heat.

Heat the olive oil and saute the tomatoes and onions for 2 minutes. Add the mushrooms and saute 2 minutes more. Start cooking the pasta (angel hair pasta only takes about 2-3 minutes in boiling water).

Season the tomato mixture with the parsley, oregano, pepper, garlic and basil. When the pasta is done, rinse and drain.

Toss the pasta in the cheese sauce. Serve topped with the tomato mixture and sprinkle the parmesan over each serving.

Nutrition information per serving: Calories: 238

Complex carbohydrates:	66%	Fat:	14%
Protein:	18%	Saturated fat:	4%
Iron:	4 mg	Monounsaturated fat:	7%
Calcium:	131 mg	Polyunsaturated fat:	3%
Potassium:	674 mg	Cholesterol:	0 mg
Fiber:	4 gm	Sodium:	91 mg

Pasta & Crab with Vegetables

Serves 4
25 Minutes

When you're in a hurry and need a one-dish meal, try this one. Serve with a salad and bread.

12	ounces spiral pasta	1	tablespoon parsley
1	teaspoon olive oil	1	cup peas (if frozen - thaw)
1	cup onion, chopped	1	cup mushrooms, chopped
2	teaspoons garlic	6	ounces crab, cut into bite-size pieces
2	teaspoons margarine, low fat	1	cup tomatoes, chopped
2	teaspoons flour	1	teaspoon worchestershire sauce,
3	tablespoons skim milk		low-salt
1/4	cup white wine	1/2	teaspoon lemon juice
1/4	teaspoon pepper	1	tablespoon parmesan cheese, grated
1	tablespoon basil		

Cook the pasta, rinse, drain and set aside.

In a large skillet coated with cooking spray, heat the olive oil and saute the onion and garlic. Add the margarine, flour, milk and wine. Stir until smooth. Add the seasonings, peas, mushrooms and crab. Simmer 3 minutes. Add the tomatoes, worchestershire sauce and lemon juice. Simmer 2 minutes more.

Toss the pasta with the sauce and serve topped with parmesan cheese.

Nutrition information per serving:

Calories: 387

Complex carbohydrates:	63%	Fat:	12%
Protein:	21%	Saturated fat:	3%
Iron:	4 mg	Monounsaturated fat:	6%
Calcium:	94 mg	Polyunsaturated fat:	3%
Potassium:	604 mg	Cholesterol:	0 mg
Fiber:	5 gm	Sodium:	392 mg

Pasta in Tomato Wine Sauce

Serves 4
35 Minutes

You may want to add a small amount of meat to this dish, but it is terrific by itself.

1/2	cup mushrooms, sliced		1	bay leaf
1/2	cup onion, chopped		1/2	cup red wine
1/2	teaspoon olive oil		Dash salt	
1/4	teaspoon garlic		Dash pepper	
1	teaspoon basil		1/2	teaspoon worchestershire sauce, low sodium
1	tablespoon parsley			
1/2	tablespoon oregano		1/2	pound fettucini noodles
2/3	cup water		2	tablespoons romano cheese, grated
6	ounces tomato paste, low salt		3	tablespoons parmesan cheese, grated
1/2	teaspoon lemon juice			

In a large non-stick skillet, saute the mushrooms and onion in the oil, seasoning with the garlic, basil, parsley and oregano. When onions are tender, add the water, paste, lemon juice, bay leaf, wine and worchestershire sauce. Simmer 20 minutes or more.

Cook the fettucini. Add fettucini to the sauce, stirring well and toss with the romano. Serve topped with parmesan.

Nutrition information per serving: Calories: 270

Complex carbohydrates:	57%	Fat:	18%
Protein:	20%	Saturated fat:	9%
Iron:	3 mg	Monounsaturated fat:	7%
Calcium:	184 mg	Polyunsaturated fat:	2%
Potassium:	641 mg	Cholesterol:	104 mg
Fiber:	3 gm	Sodium:	345 mg

Lasagna

The original recipe this one is based on was given by my friend, Ms. Colangelo. This version has spinach added for flavor.

8	ounces extra lean ground beef or turkey	1/2	teaspoon oregano
		16	ounces lasagna noodles
1/2	teaspoon olive oil	10	ounces spinach (if frozen - thaw)
1/2	teaspoon garlic	1/4	cup cottage cheese, low fat
4	16 ounce cans whole tomatoes	2/3	cup ricotta cheese, low fat
3	tablespoons tomato paste	3/4	cup mozzarella cheese, low fat
1	cup mushrooms, chopped	3/4	cup egg substitute
2	tablespoons parsley	2	tablespoons romano cheese, grated
1	tablespoon basil	2	tablespoons parmesan cheese, grated

In a large skillet coated with cooking spray, brown the meat and garlic. Add the tomatoes, paste, mushrooms and herbs. Simmer 20 minutes. Cook the lasagna. Set aside.

Mix the cottage cheese, ricotta and mozzarella cheeses with the egg substitute. In a 9" square pan coated with cooking spray, spread 1/3 of the sauce, then a layer of 1/2 of the noodles, then 1/2 of the spinach, sprinkle 1/2 of the meat, then 1/2 of the cheeses. Sprinkle with the romano cheese.

Make another layer of sauce, noodles, spinach, meat and cheeses. Top with remaining sauce and sprinkle parmesan over top. Bake covered at 350 degrees for 30 minutes.

Nutrition information per serving: Calories: 268

Complex carbohydrates:	42%	Fat:	26%
Protein:	31%	Saturated fat:	14%
Iron:	4 mg	Monunsaturated fat:	10%
Calcium:	270 mg	Polyunsaturated fat:	3%
Potassium:	568 mg	Cholesterol:	33 mg
Fiber:	4 gm	Sodium:	260 mg

Mini Pizzas

Serves 4 (2 muffin halves per serving)
15 Minutes

When you are in a hurry and need a quick dinner or filling snack, try this recipe.

2	tablespoons tomato paste	1/2	cup mushrooms, sliced
1	tablespoon onion, minced	1/3	cup onion, chopped
8	ounces canned tomatoes	1/2	teaspoon oregano
1/2	teaspoon garlic	1/3	cup mozzarella, low fat, shredded
4	wheat english muffins	1	teaspoon basil

In a sauce pan, mix the paste, onion, tomatoes and garlic. Simmer 5 minutes.

Lightly toast the english muffins. Spread the sauce over each half. Top with mushrooms, onion and oregano. Sprinkle the cheese and basil over the tops.

Broil each muffin half until the cheese melts (2-3 minutes).

Nutrition information per serving: Calories: 189

Complex carbohydrates:	59%	Fat:	15%
Protein:	21%	Saturated fat:	7%
Iron:	2 mg	Monounsaturated fat:	5%
Calcium:	147 mg	Polyunsaturated fat:	3%
Potassium:	553 mg	Cholesterol:	8 mg
Fiber:	3 gm	Sodium:	278 mg

Easy Cheese Pizza

Serves 4 (2 slices per serving)
20 Minutes

If you prefer to keep frozen pizzas handy for a quick dinner, try this recipe to get more complex carbohydrates. Add whatever vegetables you like. Be aware, though, that, as with most packaged commercial foods, the average frozen pizza is extremely high in sodium.

1	10" frozen cheese pizza	1/3	cup artichokes, chopped (optional)
1/3	cup onion, chopped	1	teaspoon oregano
1/2	cup mushrooms, chopped	1	teaspoon basil
1/2	cup green pepper, chopped	1/4	cup mozzarella, low fat, shredded

Spread the onion, mushrooms, green pepper and artichokes over the frozen pizza. Sprinkle the top with the herbs and cheese.

Bake according to package directions, usually 400 degrees for 10 minutes.

Nutrition information per serving: Calories: 274

Complex carbohydrates:	53%	Fat:	25%
Protein:	17%	Saturated fat:	10%
Iron:	2 mg	Monounsaturated fat:	11%
Calcium:	215mg	Polyunsaturated fat:	4%
Potassium:	258 mg	Cholesterol:	27 mg
Fiber:	3 gm	Sodium:	674 mg

POULTRY

Oven-fried Chicken

Serves 4
1 Hour
(10 M Preparation)

The all-American favorite can be healthy and *have the taste you want.* And *it's easy to prepare.*

1	pound chicken breasts	1/4	cup skim milk
1/2	cup corn flakes	1	tablespoon parsley
3	tablespoons almonds, crushed	1/2	teaspoon pepper

Mix the corn flakes with the almonds. Dip the chicken in the milk and coat with the corn flake mixture. Place the chicken in a baking dish coated with cooking spray.

Bake at 400 degrees for 30 minutes. Turn, bake for another 20-25 minutes more.

Nutrition information per serving: Calories: 167

Complex carbohydrates:	11%	Fat:	27%
Protein:	58%	Saturated fat:	5%
Iron:	1 mg	Monounsaturated fat:	15%
Calcium:	46 mg	Polyunsaturated fat:	6%
Potassium:	250 mg	Cholesterol:	58 mg
Fiber:	1 gm	Sodium:	94 mg

Chicken Stir-fry

Serves 4
30 Minutes
(15 M Preparation)

A fast, easy chicken dinner with vegetables, too. Serve with rice for a complete dinner.

16	ounces chicken breast	1	carrot, peeled, sliced
2	tablespoons cornstarch	1	stalk celery, sliced
2	tablespooons sherry	1/2	cup bean sprouts (optional)
2	teaspoons soy sauce, low sodium	1/2	cup mushrooms, sliced
1	teaspoon canola oil	1/4	teaspoon ginger
1	cup onion, sliced	1/2	teaspoon garlic
2	green onions, sliced	4	ounces waterchestnuts

Trim the chicken of all visible fat and remove skin. Cut into bite-size pieces. Place chicken in a glass bowl. Sprinkle the chicken with the cornstarch and add the sherry and soy sauce. Toss the chicken in the sauces and marinate in the refrigerator for 15 minutes.

In a large skillet coated with cooking spray, saute the chicken 2-3 minutes. (Save the marinade.) Add the oil, onions, carrot, celery, sprouts and mushrooms.

Saute the vegetables with the chicken 3 minutes more (for crispy vegetables) or longer (for tender vegetables). Add the marinade, seasonings and waterchestnuts. Cook 2 minutes more. Serve with rice.

Nutrition information per serving: Calories: 264

Complex carbohydrates:	21%	Fat:	16%
Protein:	59%	Saturated fat:	5%
Iron:	2 mg	Monounsaturated fat:	8%
Calcium:	44 mg	Polyunsturated fat:	4%
Potassium:	567 mg	Cholesterol:	96 mg
Fiber:	3 gm	Sodium:	218 mg

Coq au Vin

Serves 4
1 Hour
(15 M Preparation)

A french classic, chicken in wine sauce is a gourmet dish that's easy to prepare and has a rich taste.

1	slice bacon, low salt cooked very crisp	1/2	teaspoon thyme
3/4	cup onion, chopped	1	tablespoon basil
1/2	teaspoon garlic	2	tablespoon parsley
1/2	teaspoon canola oil	1/2	teaspoon pepper
1	pound chicken breasts	1/2	cup chicken broth
2	tablespoons flour	1/2	cup white wine
		1	cup mushrooms, sliced

To cook the bacon crisp, use the microwave. Saute the crumbled bacon, onion and garlic in the oil. Set the mixture aside.

Using the same skillet, brown the chicken on both sides. Stir in the flour and herbs. Add the broth, wine and bacon mixture. Heat to a boil.

Transfer the chicken to a baking dish coated with cooking spray. Pour the sauce over the chicken and bake at 350 degrees for 35 minutes. Add the mushrooms and continue baking 10 minutes more.

Nutrition information per serving:
Calories: 189

Complex carbohydrates:	15%	Fat:	16%
Protein:	59%	Saturated fat:	5%
Iron:	2 mg	Monounsturated fat:	7%
Calcium:	45 mg	Polyunsaturated fat:	4%
Potassium:	387 mg	Cholesterol:	67 mg
Fiber:	1 gm	Sodium:	96 mg

Chicken Florentine

Serves 4
45 Minutes
(15 M Preparation)

A great recipe from my sister Kylene. The spinach adds flavor to the chicken. The bacon rounds out the taste, just be sure to cook the bacon very crisp. Serve this with rice and steamed vegetables.

4	4 -ounce chicken breasts, boneless	1	teaspoon basil
1	cup spinach, chopped	1/4	teaspoon nutmeg
1/2	cup mushrooms, sliced	2/3	cup mozzarella cheese, low fat, shredded
3/4	cup onion, chopped	1	slice bacon, low salt, very crisp
1/2	teaspoon lemon juice	1	teaspoon olive oil
1/4	cup teaspoon garlic	1	tablespoon parsley

Remove the skin from the chicken and trim all visible fat. Pound the chicken very flat.

Cook the spinach (if frozen, microwave 3-4 minutes). Drain thoroughly. Saute the mushrooms and onion in a skillet coated with cooking spray. Mix in the spinach, lemon juice, garlic, nutmeg and basil.

Spoon the spinach mixture onto each chicken breast. Top with cheese and crumbled bacon and roll up. Heat the olive oil and brown the chicken on each side.

Place the chicken in a baking dish coated with cooking spray and top with parsley. Bake at 350 degrees for 30 minutes.

Nutrition information per serving: Calories: 273

Complex carbohydrates:	8%	Fat:	25%
Protein:	64%	Saturated fat:	10%
Iron:	2 mg	Monounsturated fat:	11%
Potassium:	542 mg	Polyunsaturated fat:	4%
Calcium:	199 mg	Cholesterol:	106 mg
Fiber:	2 gm	Sodium:	235 mg

Chicken Almondine

Serves 4
20 Minutes

Whether you prepare this with chicken , turkey or veal, it has a light, delicate taste. It's rewarding to have a meal as good as this in 20 minutes.

4	4 ounce chicken breasts <u>or</u> turkey breasts or veal cutlets	1/2	cup onion, chopped
3	tablespoons skim milk	1	teaspoon lemon juice
2	tablespoons wheat flour	1	tablespoon brandy
1	teaspoon olive oil	2	teaspoon worchestershire sauce, low sodium
1/4	teaspoon pepper	2	tablespoons water
2	teaspoons basil	1	tablespoon flour
1	tablespoon parsley	1	tablespoon almonds, sliced
11/2	cup mushrooms, sliced		Parsley

Pound the chicken very thin and dredge in the milk, then the flour. Place the chicken in a skillet coated with cooking spray. Brown 2-3 minutes each side, seasoning with the herbs and pepper. Transfer to a non-stick baking dish. Place the dish in a 300 degree oven for 5 to 8 minutes.

Saute the mushrooms and onion in the juice, brandy and worchestershire sauce. Mix the flour with the water and add to the vegetable mixture. Cook 1 minute over high heat.

Pour the sauce over the chicken, sprinkle with almonds and broil for 1-2 minutes. Serve topped with parsley.

Nutrition information per serving:

Calories: 141

Complex carbohydrates:	17%	Fat:	16%
Protein:	60%	Saturated fat:	4%
Iron:	1 mg	Monounsaturated fat:	8%
Calcium:	35 mg	Polyunsturated fat:	4%
Potassium:	332 mg	Cholesterol:	50 mg
Fiber:	1 gm	Sodium:	70 mg

Arroz con Pollo (Chicken with Rice)

Serves 4
1 Hour
(15 M Preparation)

The original of this wonderful combination dinner is from my friend Ms. Guererro from Puerto Rico. It offers an easy way to fix your meat and rice together - just add vegetables!

2	teaspoons canola oil	2	cups water
1	cup onion, chopped	1/2	teaspoon garlic
1/2	cup green pepper, chopped	3/4	cup tomato sauce, no salt added
2	teaspoon capers (optional)	1	cup rice (not pre-cooked)
14	ounces boneless chicken breasts	1	cup peas
1	teaspoon pepper		

Heat the oil in a large skillet and add the onion, peppers and capers.

Remove the skin from the chicken, trim all fat and cut into bite-size pieces. Add the chicken to the skillet mixture, season with pepper and add the water, garlic and tomato sauce.

Cook covered for at least 25 minutes over low heat. Add the rice and peas. Cover and continue to cook over low heat 20 minutes.

Nutrition information per serving:　　Calories: 222

Complex carbohydrates:	35%	Fat:	20%
Protein:	41%	Saturated fat:	4%
Iron:	2 mg	Monounsaturated fat:	11%
Calcium:	46 mg	Polyunsaturated fat:	5%
Potassium:	438 mg	Cholesterol:	49 mg
Fiber:	4 gm	Sodium:	264 mg

Fajitas in a Pita

Serves 4 (2 pita pockets per serving)
30 Minutes

Fajitas are so good, but they're even better prepared this way. You will find that serving them in a pita makes them easier to eat as well as healthier.

1/2	teaspoon garlic	1	cup onion, chopped
1	tablespoon canola oil	1	teaspoon canola oil
1	tablespoon lemon juice	4	pita pockets, wheat, cut in half
1	drop hot sauce (or to taste)	1/4	cup salsa, low salt
1/2	teaspoon pepper	1/2	cup plain yogurt, non-fat
2	teaspoons worchershire sauce, low sodium	1	cup tomatoes, chopped
		1	cup lettuce, shredded
2	tablespoons white wine	1/2	cup cheddar cheese, low fat,
1	pound chicken breasts, boneless		shredded

Combine the garlic, oil, juice, hot sauce, pepper, worchershire sauce and wine. Remove the skin and fat from the chicken and cut into bite-size pieces. Marinate the chicken refrigerated for 15 minutes.

Saute the onion in the oil until tender. Heat the pitas in the oven at 250 degrees for 10 minutes. Place the yogurt, tomatoes, lettuce and cheese in individual small bowls to be used for garnish on your fajita.

Place the chicken and onions on a broiler pan and broil 4 inches away from heat for 5 minutes. Serve the chicken and onions on a warm plate, and the pitas also on a warm plate. Let everyone put their *fajita pitas* together according to their own tastes.

Nutrition information per serving:

Calories: 431

Complex carbohydrates:	32%	Fat:	19%
Protein:	44%	Saturated fat:	6%
Iron:	3 mg	Monounsaturated fat:	8%
Calcium:	182 mg	Polyunsaturated fat:	5%
Potassium:	707 mg	Cholesterol:	102 mg
Fiber:	6 gm	Sodium:	580 mg

Oriental Chicken with Rice

Serves 4
25 Minutes
(15 M Preparation)

Similar to Arroz con Pollo, *this meal combines the meat with the rice and vegetables so you have less to prepare and less mess!*

2	cups chicken broth. low sodium	1/2	cup peas
		3/4	cup carrot, sliced
1	cup uncooked rice	3	tablespoons sherry
8	ounces chicken breasts, boneless	2	teaspoons soy sauce, low sodium

Combine the broth and rice. Cover and simmer 20 minutes.

Remove the skin and fat from the chicken and cut into bite-size pieces. Saute in a skillet coated with cooking spray. Add the peas, carrot, sherry and soy sauce. Cover and simmer 10-15 minutes. (The vegetables will be crisp)

Serve the chicken and vegetables over the rice.

Nutrition information per serving: Calories: 177

Complex carbphydrates:	46%	Fat:	10%
Protein:	39%	Saturated fat:	3%
Iron:	1 mg	Monounsaturated fat:	4%
Calcium:	32 mg	Polyunsaturated fat:	3%
Potassium:	319 mg	Cholesterol:	33 mg
Fiber:	3 gm	Sodium:	206 mg

Chicken Teriyaki Broil

Serves 4
30 Minute
(10 M Preparation)

The Teriyaki Broil *is quick and very easy to make. It makes a delicious meal after a hard day.*

1	pound chicken breasts boneless	1/2	cup pineapple juice
2	tablespoons sherry	2	tablespoons soy sauce. low sodium
1/2	teaspoon garlic	3	tablespoons sesame oil
		1/2	teaspoon ginger

Remove the skin from the chicken and trim all visible fat. Cut the chicken into bite-size pieces.

Combine the sherry, garlic, juice, soy sauce, oil and ginger in a glass bowl. Marinate the chicken in the sauce for 20 minutes.

Place the chicken on a broiling pan coated with cooking spray. Baste with marinade. Broil 4" from the heat for 3-4 minutes each side.

Nutrition information per serving:

		Calories: 248	
Complex carbohydrates:	8%	Fat:	25%
Protein:	62%	Saturated fat:	6%
Iron:	2 mg	Monounsaturated fat:	10%
Calcium:	23 mg	Polyunsaturated fat:	8%
Potassium:	361 mg	Cholesterol:	96 mg
Fiber:	0 gm	Sodium:	236 mg

Baked Chicken

Serves 4
55 Minutes
(15 M Preparation)

A very easy family favorite. The preparation is simple and the baking time allows time to relax!

4	boneless chicken breast	1	teaspoon basil
1/2	cup egg substitute	1/4	teaspoon salt
1	cup skim milk	1/4	teaspoon pepper
1	cup wheat flour	1	tablespoon parsley
1	teaspoon olive oil		

Remove the skin from the chicken and trim all visible fat. In a shallow bowl, mix the egg substitute and milk. Place the flour in another shallow bowl.

Heat the olive oil in a large skillet. Dredge the chicken in the egg mixture, then the flour mixture and brown in the skillet. Turn and brown on both sides.

Place the chicken in a baking dish coated with cooking spray. Bake at 350 degrees for 45 minutes. Serve topped with parsley.

Nutrition information per serving: Calories: 261

Complex carbohydartes:	18%	Fat:	17%
Protein:	63%	Saturated fat:	5%
Iron:	2 mg	Monounsaturated fat:	8%
Calcium:	34 mg	Polyunsaturated fat:	4%
Potassium:	382 mg	Cholesterol:	97 mg
Fiber:	2 gm	Sodium:	109 mg

Chicken & Crab Rolls

Serves 4
45 Minutes
(30 M Preparation)

An impressive entree to serve your favorite people. It has a smooth, buttery taste without all the fat.

4	4 ounce chicken breasts	1	tablespoon parmesan <u>or</u> blue cheese
1/2	cup onion, chopped	3	tablespoons skim milk
3/4	cup mushrooms, chopped	1	tablespoon plain yogurt, non-fat
1	teaspoon margarine, low fat	1/3	cup almonds, crushed
1/2	cup imitation crab	1/2	cup oat bran
1/3	cup egg substitute	Parsley	
1	egg white		

Remove the skin from the chicken and trim all visible fat. Pound the chicken very thin.

Saute the onion, mushrooms and crab in a skillet coated with cooking spray. Fold in the egg substitute, egg white and cheese. Spread the mixture on each piece of chicken, top with a teaspoon of yogurt. Roll the chicken up, enveloping the mixture.

Mix the almonds and oat bran in a shallow bowl. Holding the chicken rolls carefully, dip them in the milk and then the almond mixture. Place in a shallow baking dish and brown over medium heat (approximately 2 minutes each side).

Bake at 325 degrees for 15 minutes. Serve topped with parsley.

Nutrition information per serving:

		Calories: 265	
Complex carbohydrates:	21%	Fat	21%
Protein:	47%	Saturated fat:	6%
Iron:	2 mg	Monounsaturated fat:	16%
Calcium:	89 mg	Polyunsaturated fat:	8%
Potassium:	469 mg	Cholesterol:	57 mg
Fiber:	3 gm	Sodium:	240 mg

Island Chicken

Serves 4
1 Hour
(15 M Preparation)

The tangy taste of this chicken is reminiscent of the tastes of the caribbean.

1	teaspoon olive oil	1	tablespoon wine
1	tablespoon worchestershire sauce, low sodium	1	teaspoon mustard
		1	teaspoon margarine, low fat
3	green onions, chopped	1	pound chicken breasts, boneless
1	tablespoon flour	1/2	teaspoon curry powder
1/2	cup water		

In a large non-stick skillet, saute the oil, worchestershire sauce and onions over low heat until tender. Stir in the flour, water, wine, mustard, and margarine over low heat until smooth.

Remove the skin, trim the fat and place the chicken in a baking dish coated with cooking spray and pour the mixture over it. Sprinkle the curry over the chicken. Cover and bake at 375 degrees for 35-40 minutes. Baste with the sauce every 15 minutes.

Nutrition information per serving: Calories: 196

Complex carbohydrates:	8%	Fat:	20%
Protein;	69%	Saturated fat:	5%
Iron:	1 mg	Monounsturated fat:	10%
Calcium:	22 mg	Polyunsaturated fat:	4%
Potassium:	334 mg	Cholesterol:	84 mg
Fiber:	1 gm	Sodium:	149 mg

Turkey-Cheese Crescents

Serves 4
45 Minutes
(20 M Preparation)

These crescents can be made with turkey breasts or veal cutlets. Either way, you will enjoy their unique taste.

4	4-ounce turkey breasts	1	tablespoon basil
	or	1/4	cup egg substitute
4	4-ounce veal cutlets	2	tablespoons skim milk
2/3	cup monterey jack cheese low fat, shredded	31/2	tablespoons oat bran
		2	tablespoons, almonds, crushed
1/4	teaspoon pepper	1	teaspoon margarine, low fat
1/4	teaspoon sage	1	teaspoon canola oil

Flatten the meat to very thin. Sprinkle the cheese on each piece of meat. Season with the pepper, sage and basil. Fold the cutlets over and pound the edges to seal.

Mix the egg substitute and milk in a shallow bowl. In another shallow bowl, combine the oat bran and almonds. Dredge the crescents in the egg mixture, then in the almond mixture to coat thoroughly.

Heat the margarine and oil and brown the meat on both sides. Place the meat in a baking dish coated with cooking spray. Bake at 350 degrees for 20-25 minutes.

Nutrition information per serving:

Calories: 234

Complex carbohydrates:	7%	Fat:	28%
Protein:	62%	Saturated fat:	13%
Iron:	2 mg	Monounsaturated fat:	13%
Calcium:	148 mg	Polyunsaturated fat:	3%
Potassium:	369 mg	Cholesterol:	89 mg
Fiber:	1 gm	Sodium:	151 mg

Turkey Sloppy Joes

Makes 12 Sandwiches
1 1/4 Hour
(15 M Preparation)

My father's favorite. You will be surprised at how much these taste like sloppy joes made with beef!

2	pounds ground turkey (or extra lean beef)	1	stalk celery, chopped
18	ounces ketchup, low salt	1/4	teaspoon pepper
8	ounces tomato sauce, low salt	1/2	teaspoon oregano
1/2	cup onion, chopped	1	teaspoon chives
1/4	teaspoon worchestershire sauce, low sodium	1	teaspoon basil
		12	Hamburger buns, whole grain

Brown the meat in a non-stick skillet. Add the ketchup, tomato sauce, onion, worchestershire sauce, celery and season to taste.

Simmer 1 hour. Serve on whole grain buns.

Nutrition information per serving: Calories: 283

Complex carbohydrates:	30%	Fat:	17%
Protein:	41%	Saturated fat:	5%
Iron:	1 mg	Monounsaturated fat:	6%
Calcium:	34 mg	Polyunsaturated fat:	7%
Potassium:	569 mg	Cholesterol:	58 mg
Fiber:	6 gm	Sodium:	478 mg

SEAFOOD

Japanese Crab Cakes

Serves 4 (3 cakes each)
20 Minutes

The "Surimi" or imitation crab is easily kept in the freezer for when you need a quick dinner. These cakes are very easy and exceptionally good!

10	ounces imitation crab	1	cup mushrooms
1	cup frozen peas		Dash of ginger
3/4	cup egg substitute	2	teaspoons basil
1/2	cup onion, chopped	2	teaspoons canola oil
1/3	cup green pepper (optional)	1	teaspoon soy sauce, low sodium

Chop the crab, peas, onion, green pepper, mushrooms in a food processor for 5 seconds or just until coarsely chopped. Mix with the egg substitute, ginger and basil.

Heat the oil in a large skillet. Pour the batter into the skillet, forming 3" circles. Sprinkle each with soy sauce. Fry 3-4 minutes each side, turning carefully.

Serve with steamed vegetables and rice.

Nutrition information per serving: Calories: 151

Complex carbohydartes:	44%	Fat:	13%
Protein:	35%	Saturated fat:	2%
Iron:	1 mg	Monounsaturated fat:	10%
Calcium:	15 mg	Polyunsaturated fat:	2%
Potassium:	118 mg	Cholesterol:	2 mg
Fiber:	1 gm	Sodium:	167 mg

Crab and Artichokes

Serves 4
35 Minutes
(20 M Preparation)

The artichokes in this dish add a lot of flavor. You may want to try it with other vegetables, too.

14	ounces artichoke hearts, frozen or canned	21/2	tablespoons flour
		1/4	teaspoon salt
11/2	cup mushrooms, sliced	1	tablespoon sherry
10	ounces imitation crab	2	tablespoons wheat germ
2/3	cup skim milk	1	tablespoon parmesan cheese
2	tablespoons dry skim milk		

Place the artichoke hearts in the bottom of a casserole dish coated with cooking spray. Then add a layer of crab, then a layer of mushrooms.

Mix the milk, dry milk, flour and salt in a sauce pan. Cook over a low heat, stirring with a whisk until thick and smooth. Add the sherry. Pour the sauce over the crab mixture.

In a separate bowl, combine the wheat germ with the parmesan and sprinkle over the casserole. Bake at 400 degrees for 12-15 minutes.

Nutrition information per serving: Calories: 171

Complex carbohydrates:	56%	Fat:	4%
Protein:	33%	Saturated fat:	2%
Iron:	2 mg	Monounsaturated fat:	1%
Calcium:	142 mg	Polyunsaturated fat:	1%
Potassium:	541 mg	Cholesterol:	9 mg
Fiber:	3 gm	Sodium:	323 mg

Sole with Vegetables

Serves 4
30 Minutes
(15 M Preparaton)

Sole is a light fish with very little "fishy" taste when prepared in a sauce such as this. Fish is not only very low in fat, but quick and easy to prepare.

2	tablespoons white wine
1/4	cup chicken broth
1/2	cup mushrooms, sliced
1/2	cup onion, chopped
1/2	cup tomatoes, chopped
4	sole fillets, 4 ounces each
2	teaspoons canola oil
1	tablespoon basil
1/4	teaspoon pepper
1/4	cup egg substitute
1/3	cup monterey jack cheese, low fat shredded
1	tablespoon parmesan cheese

Heat the wine and broth and saute the mushrooms and onion until tender. Add the tomatoes, basil and pepper. Gradually blend in the egg substitute and heat for 1 minute more.

Place the fillets in a baking dish coated with cooking spray. Pour the sauce over the fillets and sprinkle the cheeses over the top. Bake at 350 degrees for 12 minutes. Then broil for 3-4 minutes until the cheese melts.

Nutrition information per serving: Calories: 195

Complex carbohydrates:	7%	Fat:	23%
Protein:	63%	Saturated fat:	9%
Iron:	2 mg	Monounsaturated fat:	9%
Calcium:	128 mg	Polyunsaturated fat:	5%
Potassium:	720 mg	Cholesterol:	85 mg
Fiber:	1 gm	Sodium:	205 mg

Caribbean Sole

Serves 4
50 Minutes
(10 M Preparation)

Preparing fruit with fish not only gives the fish more flavor, it adds fiber and complex carbohydrates. Use whatever fruit you prefer.

1	banana, sliced	4	fillets of sole or orange roughy
1/2	cup pineapple or grapefruit	11/2	tablespoons brown sugar
1/4	cup orange juice	1/2	teaspoon cinnamon
1	tablespoon grand marnier or brandy		

Combine the fruit, juice and liquor in a glass bowl. Marinate the fillets for 30 minutes. Place the fish in a baking dish coated with cooking spray.

Pour the liquid marinade over the fish. Bake at 350 degrees for 10 minutes.

Lay the fruit slices over the fish, basting again with the marinade. Sprinkle the brown sugar and cinnamon over the top. Broil for 1-2 minutes. Serve with rice.

Nutrition information per serving: Calories: 161

Complex carbohydrates:	25%	Fat:	6%
Protein:	54%	Saturated fat:	2%
Iron:	1mg	Monounsaturated fat:	1%
Calcium:	32 mg	Polyunsaturated fat:	2%
Potassium:	472 mg	Cholesterol:	56 mg
Fiber:	1 gm	Sodium:	89 mg

Salmon L'Orange

Serves 4
1 Hour
(10 M Preparation)

The marinating of the fish gives it a light, delicate flavor without salt and makes it taste less "fishy".

1/2	cup orange juice	1	teaspoon worchestershire sauce
1	tablespoon Grand Marnier	4	salmon fillets, 4 ounces each
2	tablespoons canola oil	Parsley	

Combine the juice, liquor, oil and worchestershire sauce in a glass bowl. Marinate the fillets for 30 minutes in the refrigerator.

Place the fish in a baking dish coated with cooking spray. Pour the marinade over the fish. Bake at 400 degrees for 20 minutes, basting frequently.

Serve topped with marinade sauce and parsley.

Nutrition information per serving: Calories: 147

Complex carbohydrates:	9%	Fat:	32%
Protein:	58%	Saturated fat:	6%
Iron:	1 mg	Monounsatuirated fat:	13%
Calcium:	14 mg	Polyunsaturated fat:	13%
Potassium:	386 mg	Cholesterol:	51 mg
Fiber:	0 gm	Sodium:	75 mg

Tuna Oriental

If you've ever had fresh tuna, you know what a delicate taste it has. The sauce gives an even better variation.

1	teaspoon margarine, low fat	1/2	cup chicken broth
1/2	cup mushrooms, sliced	1	tablespoon soy sauce, low sodium
1/2	cup peas	1	teaspoon cornstarch
1/4	cup green onion, chopped	4	tuna fillets, 4 ounces each
1	teaspoon ginger	1	teaspoon canola oil
1/2	teaspoon garlic	1	tablespoon sliced almonds

In a large skillet, heat the margarine. Saute the mushrooms, peas and onions until tender, seasoning with the ginger and garlic. Combine the broth, soy sauce and cornstarch then add to the skillet. Cook over medium-low heat until thick.

Place the tuna in a baking dish coated with cooking spray. Brush the tuna with oil and cover them with sauce. Broil 3-4 minutes, turn sprinkle almonds over the tops and broil 3-4 minutes more.

Nutrition information per serving:

Calories: 206

Complex carbohydrates:	12%	Fat:	32%
Protein:	52%	Saturated fat:	7%
Iron:	2 mg	Monounsaturated fat:	15%
Calcium:	27 mg	Polyunsaturated fat:	11%
Potassium:	517 mg	Cholesterol:	39 mg
Fiber:	1 gm	Sodium:	253 mg

Broiled Scallops

Serves 4
35 Minutes
(10 M Preparation)

Scallops have a rich flavor, especially when marinated. They are easy and quick to prepare.

1/4	cup white wine	18	ounces scallops, rinsed drained
1	tablespoon mustard	1/2	cup mushrooms
1	drop hot sauce	Parsley	
2	tablespoon honey		
1	teaspoon worchestershire sauce, low sodium		

Combine the wine, mustard, hot sauce, worchestershire sauce and scallops in a glass bowl. Marinate refrigerated for 15 minutes.

Place the scallops on a broiling pan and broil for 5 minutes. Turn and add mushrooms. Baste all with the marinade. Broil 5 minutes more. Serve topped with parsley.

Nutrition information per serving: Calories: 224

Complex carbohydrates:	11%	Fat:	4%
Protein:	68%	Saturated fat:	0%
Iron:	1 mg	Monounsaturated fat:	1%
Calcium:	58 mg	Polyunsaturated fat:	3%
Potassium:	755mg	Cholesterol:	72 mg
Fiber:	0 gm	Sodium:	348 mg

Shrimp in Tomato Sauce

Serves 4
15 Minutes

Simple and easy, this entree has great flavor. Shellfish are high in dietary cholesterol, but very low in fat. Limit your shellfish to about once a week and always serve with rice.

1	pound shrimp	1	tablespoon soy sauce, low sodium
1	8 ounce can tomato sauce	1	teaspoon chili sauce (or 1/2 teaspoon
1	teaspoon sugar		horseradish)
2	tablespoons water		

If necessary, peel and de-vein shrimp.

In a large skillet, combine the tomato sauce, sugar, water, soy sauce and chili sauce over low heat. Simmer, stirring, 2 minutes. Add shrimp and saute for 5 minutes over low heat, stirring gently.

Serve over rice.

Nutrition information per serving: Calories: 192

Complex carbohydrates:	6%	Fat:	8%
Protein:	84%	Saturated fat:	4%
Iron:	6 mg	Monounsaturated fat:	0%
Calcium:	83 mg	Polyunsaturated fat:	4%
Potassium:	513 mg	Cholesterol:	335 mg
Fiber:	2 gm	Sodium:	552 mg

Sauteed Shrimp

Serves 4
15 Minutes

Use shrimp or imitation crab in this recipe. The crab is lower in sodium and cholesterol; the shrimp has more flavor.

1	pound shrimp	1	tablespoon soy sauce, low sodium
2	teaspoons canola oil	10	ounces green beans, frozen
1	cup onions, chopped	2	tablespoons water

If necessary, peel and de-vein the shrimp. Heat the oil in a skillet and saute the shrimp for 3-4 minutes. Add the onion, soy sauce and water.

Cover and simmer 5 minutes. Serve over rice.

Nutrition information per serving: Calories: 228

Complex carbohydrates:	13%	Fat:	16%
Protein:	71%	Saturated fat:	4%
Iron:	6 mg	Monounsaturated fat:	5%
Calcium:	116 mg	Polyunsaturated fat:	6%
Potassium:	514 mg	Cholesterol:	335 mg
Fiber:	2 gm	Sodium:	485 mg

RED MEATS

Stir-Fried Beef

Serves 4
20 Minutes

This is an easy dinner with a unique taste. Try adding vegetables to the stir-fry to save additional work.

1	pound sirloin steak, lean	11/2	cup mushrooms, chopped
Dash of salt & pepper		1	cup onion, chopped
1	tablespoon flour	1/2	cup green pepper, chopped
2	teaspoons cornstarch	1	tablespoon dijon mustard
1/4	cup water	2	teaspoon basil
2	tablespoons worchestershire sauce, low sodium	Parsley	

Cut the sirloin into bite-size pieces, trimming all visible fat. (The steak will be easier to cut if still partly frozen.) Saute the meat in a large non-stick skillet with salt, pepper and flour until brown.

Combine the cornstarch, water and worchestershire sauce. In a small non-stick skillet, saute the mushrooms, onion and green pepper. Add the cornstarch mixture , mustard and basil. Add this mixture to the meat.

Cover the meat and simmer 5 minutes. Serve topped with parsley.

Nutrition information per serving:

		Calories: 158	
Complex carbohydrates:	20%	Fat:	31%
Protein:	46%	Saturated fat:	12%
Iron:	2 mg	Monounsaturated fat:	15%
Calcium:	24 mg	Polyunsaturated fat:	4%
Potassium:	425 mg	Cholesterol:	47 mg
Fiber:	1 gm	Sodium:	205 mg

173

Oriental Stir-fry

Serves 4
20 Minutes
(6 Hour marinade)

This beef stir-fry has a tangy flavor. If you plan the marinade ahead, it is a quick, easy meal to prepare.

1	pound sirloin steak	1/2	cup green pepper, chopped
2	tablespoon soy sauce, low sodium	1/2	cup mushrooms, chopped
		1/2	teaspoon garlic
3	tablespoons orange or pineapple juice	1	teaspoon canola oil
		1/2	cup onion, chopped
1/2	teaspoon ginger	1	tablespoon almonds, sliced
1	teaspoon brown sugar		

Slice the steak across the grain in bite-size pieces. Combine the soy sauce, juice, ginger and brown sugar in a glass bowl. Add the steak and refrigerate at least 6 hours.

To prepare, saute the green pepper, mushrooms, garlic and onion in the oil until tender. Add the steak pieces and almonds. Stir-fry 2-3 minutes. Add the marinade, heat 2 minutes more and serve.

Nutrition information per serving: Calories: 156

Complex carbohydrates:	10%	Fat:	32%
Protein:	55%	Saturated fat:	13%
Iron:	2 mg	Monounsaturated fat:	14%
Calcium:	12 mg	Polyunsaturated fat:	5%
Potassium:	298 mg	Cholesterol:	35 mg
Fiber:	1 gm	Sodium:	188 mg

Sukiyaki

Serves 4
20 Minutes

Sukiyaki is a great-tasting dinner that is easy and quick. My friend Chie introduced me to this and other Japanese recipes. Sukiyaki makes a simple one-dish meal.

4	cups cooked rice	2/3	cup mushrooms (shiitake preferred)
10	ounces sirloin steak, bite size, sliced very thin across grain	1	celery stalk
		10	ounces spinach, frozen or fresh
6	green onions, cut in 2" pieces	11/2	tablespoons soy sauce, low sodium
10	ounces tofu, cut in bite size pieces	1	tablespoon sugar
10	ounces oriental noodles (optional)	2	tablespoons sherry
		2/3	cup water
8	ounces waterchestnuts		

Start preparing the rice according to package directions.

Pre-heat a large non-stick skillet. Brown the meat 3-4 minutes. Add the onion, tofu, noodles, waterchestnuts, mushrooms, celery and spinach. Saute 2-3 minutes.

In a small bowl, combine the sugar, sherry, water and soy sauce. Pour a small amount into the beef mixture. Turn everything gently, simmer 3-4 minutes more.

Serve the Sukiyaki over the rice and pour sauce over all.

Nutrition information per serving: Calories: 372

Complex carbohydrates:	53%	Fat:	16%
Protein:	25%	Saturated fat:	5%
Iron:	9 mg	Monounsaturated fat:	6%
Calcium:	223 mg	Polyunsaturated fat:	5%
Potassium:	780 mg	Cholesterol:	34 mg
Fiber:	7 mg	Sodium:	310 mg

Marinated Roast Beef

Serves 4
2 Hours
(4 Hour marinade, 10 M Preparation)

Marinating the beef gives it full flavor without high sodium. Plan this meal ahead for the time needed to marinate, although it requires very little preparation time.

11/2	pound rump or chuck roast		Pepper
1	tablespoon lemon juice	1/8	teaspoon garlic
1/4	cup orange juice	1/2	cup onion, chopped
1/3	cup red wine	1/2	teaspoon canola oil
1	tablespoon basil	2	tablespoons flour

Combine the lemon juice, orange juice, wine, basil, pepper and garlic in a glass bowl.

Brown the onion in the oil until tender and add to the marinade. Add the roast and refrigerate for 4 hours or more.

Place the roast in a baking dish coated with cooking spray. Blend the flour into the marinade over low heat for a few minutes.

Then pour over the roast and bake at 350 degrees for 2 hours, basting regularly. Serve with marinade poured over each slice.

Nutrition information per serving:

Calories: 172

Complex carbohydrates:	12%	Fat:	30%
Protein:	52%	Saturated fat:	12%
Iron:	3 mg	Monounsaturated fat:	15%
Calcium:	14 mg	Polyunsaturated fat:	3%
Potassium:	263 mg	Cholesterol:	62 mg
Fiber:	0 gm	Sodium:	44 mg

Quick Roast Beef

Serves 4
1 Hour
(5 M Preparation)

This dinner is so easy to prepare and bakes quickly if you use a steak cut, as it's less thick than a regular roast.

1	pound sirloin or eye of round steak		
1	packet beef boullion, low sodium		
1	cup water	2	teaspoons parsley
1/2	teaspoon garlic	1/2	cup onion, chopped
1/2	teaspoon basil	1/2	cup mushrooms, chopped

Trim the steak of all fat and place in a non-stick baking pan. Mix the boullion and water and add to the beef. Season with the garlic, basil, parsley. Sprinkle the onions and mushrooms over.

Bake at 375 degrees for 1 hour for very done, tender meat. Baste every 15 minutes.

Nutrition information per serving: Calories: 138

Complex carbohydrates:	7%	Fat:	27%
Protein:	64%	Saturated fat:	12%
Iron:	2 mg	Monounsaturated fat:	13%
Calcium:	12 mg	Polyunsaturated fat:	3%
Potassium:	491 mg	Cholesterol:	48 mg
Fiber:	0 mg	Sodium:	47 mg

Meatloaf for the "90's"

Serves 4
11/4 Hour
(25 M Preparation)

Meatloaf has become popular again. It fits the lifestyle of busy families who need a nutritious meal that can be served anytime.

1	celery stalk	1/3	cup ketchup, low sodium
1	carrot	1	tablespoon chili sauce
1/2	cup onion	1/4	cup egg substitute
1/2	cup green pepper	1	egg white
1/2	teaspoon garlic	1/4	cup plain yogurt, non-fat
Dash salt & pepper		8	ounces extra lean ground beef
1	teaspoon basil	8	ounces ground turkey breast
1	tablespoon parsley	1/2	cup oat bran
1/4	teaspoon nutmeg	1/2	recipe "Mashed Potatoes", pg. 126
1/8	teaspoon cinnamon		

Coarsely chop the celery, carrot, onion and green pepper in a food processor. Saute the vegetables in a skillet coated with cooking spray until tender. Then spoon the vegetables into a mixing bowl.

Add seasonings to the vegetables. Toss and add ketchup, chili sauce, egg substitute, egg white, yogurt, meats and oat bran. Mix and shape into a loaf. Place the loaf on a rack in a baking dish (so the grease can drain).

Bake at 375 degrees for 30 minutes. Make the mashed potatoes and top the meatloaf with the potatoes. Bake for 15-20 minutes more.

Nutrition information per serving: Calories: 340

Complex carbohydrates:	36%	Fat:	23%
Protein:	38%	Saturated fat:	9%
Iron:	4 mg	Monounsaturated fat:	9%
Calcium:	121 mg	Polyunsaturated fat:	4%
Potassium:	909 mg	Cholesterol:	69 mg
Fiber:	5 gm	Sodium:	252 mg

Chili

Serves 8
11/2 Hour
(30 M Prepartion)

Chili is so good on a cold day. This recipe is low in fat and calories and high in taste.

1	pound extra lean ground beef	11/2	cup beef broth
1	cup onion, chopped	1/8	teaspoon cayenne pepper
2	celery stalks, chopped	1	tablespoon chili powder
8	ounces tomato sauce, low sodium	1/2	teaspoon worchestershire sauce,
1	8 ounce can kidney beans		low sodium

Brown the beef in a non-stick skillet. Drain the grease from the meat.

Stir in the onion and celery and saute a few minutes more. Then add the tomato sauce, beans, broth, pepper, chili powder and worchestershire sauce. Simmer for 1-2 hours. The longer it simmers the better it is.

Nutrition information per serving: Calories: 95

Complex carbohydrates:	30%	Fat:	9%
Protein:	56%	Saturated fat:	4%
Iron:	1 mg	Monounsaturated fat:	2%
Calcium:	29 mg	Polyunsturated fat:	3%
Potassium:	387 mg	Cholesterol:	25 mg
Fiber:	3 gm	Sodium:	150 mg

Shepherd's Pie

Serves 4
1 Hour
(30 M Preparation)

Shepherd's Pie is a one-dish meal that has been a family favorite for years. Similar to the pot pie, this version is filling but with a sauce low in fat. Try the recipe with ground turkey.

1	recipe "Mashed Potatoes" (pg. 126)	1/4	teaspoon pepper
		1/4	cup parsley
12	ounces extra lean ground beef	2	tablespoons basil
1/2	cup onion, chopped	1/2	cup chicken broth
2	carrots, chopped	2	tablespoons worchestershire sauce,
1/2	cup peas		low sodium
1/2	cup corn	1/2	tablespoon cornstarch
1/2	cup tomato, chopped	2	tablespoon water

Start cooking the potatoes for the mashed potato recipe. (Save time by microwaving the potatoes on high for 8 minutes. Be sure to prick holes in potatoes.)

In a large, non-stick skillet brown the beef then drain the fat off. Add the carrots, peas, corn, tomatoes, pepper, parsley, broth and worchestershire sauce. Simmer 20 minutes.

Mix the cornstarch with the water and add to the meat mixture. Pour the mixture into individual baking dishes or a large baking dish . Top with mashed potatoes.

Bake at 350 degrees for 30 minutes.

Nutrition information per serving: Calories: 315

Complex carbohydrates:	47%	Fat:	24%
Protein:	26%	Saturated fat:	11%
Iron:	4 mg	Monounsaturated fat:	11%
Calcium:	86 mg	Polyunsaturated fat:	2%
Potassium:	1013 mg	Cholesterol:	53 mg
Fiber:	6 gm	Sodium:	161 mg

Veal Lemon

Serves 4
20 minutes

This veal has a nice, light flavor. This dish is best complimented with steamed vegetables and rice.

4	4-ounces veal cutlets		1/4	cup white wine
1	teaspoon canola oil		1	tablespoon lemon juice
1	teaspoon basil		1	cup mushrooms, sliced
1/4	teaspoon pepper		1	tablespoons almonds, sliced
1	teaspoon cornstarch			

Pound the cutlets until very thin. Saute in the oil 3-5 minutes over medium heat on each side. Season with the basil and pepper. Mix the cornstarch with the wine.

Add the wine, lemon juice and mushrooms to the veal. Stir the veal with the sauce and saute 2 minutes or more. Serve topped with almonds.

Nutrition information per serving: Calories: 167

Complex carbohydrates:	8%	Fat:	42%
Protein:	38%	Saturated fat:	17%
Iron:	2 mg	Monounsaturated fat:	21%
Calcium:	19 mg	Polyunsaturated fat:	4%
Potassium:	327 mg	Cholesterol:	52 mg
Fiber:	1 gm	Sodium:	49 mg

Veal Crescents in Wine Sauce

Serves 4
35 Minutes
(20 M Preparation)

Whenever you include a vegetable with your meat preparation, you save time and effort. Try experimenting with your own favorites, adding complimenting vegetables.

12	ounces veal cutlets	1/2	cup chicken broth, low sodium
10	ounces spinach, frozen	21/2	tablespoons flour
1/2	teaspoon soy sauce, low sodium	2	tablespoons Butter Buds
		1/4	cup white wine
1/4	cup mozzarella, low fat, shredded		

Pound the veal cutlets until very thin. Cook the spinach lightly (if frozen, microwave for 4 minutes). Drain thoroughly.

Spoon 1/4 of the spinach onto each cutlet. Sprinkle the soy sauce and mozzarella over each. Fold each cutlet over to enclose the filling and pound the edges to seal. Place the cutlets in a baking dish coated with cooking spray.

Over low heat, combine the chicken broth, flour, Butter Buds and wine. Stir with a whisk until smooth. Pour the sauce over the cutlets and bake at 400 degrees for 10-15 minutes.

Nutrition information per serving: Calories: 183

Complex carbohydrates:	17%	Fat:	31%
Protein:	29%	Saturated fat:	16%
Iron:	3 mg	Monounsaturated fat:	14%
Calcium:	151 mg	Polyunsaturated fat:	2%
Potassium:	551 mg	Cholesterol:	47 mg
Fiber:	3 gm	Sodium:	172 mg

Lamb L'Orange

This lamb will melt in your mouth. The sauce in which it is cooked takes most of the "gamey" taste away and adds so much flavor.

20	ounces lamb chops	1	tablespoon flour
	or	3	tablespoons brown sugar
16	ounces leg of lamb	2	tablespoons lemon juice
1/4	cup balsamic vinegar	1/2	teaspoon ginger
1	cup orange juice	1	orange, sliced
1/4	cup water		

Trim the lamb of all visible fat. Brown in a skillet coated with cooking spray, turning to brown on both sides. Drain the fat and transfer the lamb to a baking dish coated with cooking spray.

In the skillet over low heat, mix the vinegar, juice, water and flour. Whisk until smooth. Then add the brown sugar, lemon juice and ginger. Pour this sauce over the lamb.

Bake uncovered at 350 degrees for 45 minutes. Baste occasionally with the sauce. Serve decorated with the sliced oranges.

Nutrition information per serving:

Calories: 302

Complex carbohydrates:	15%	Fat:	28%
Protein:	44%	Saturated fat:	13%
Iron:	3 mg	Monounsaturated fat:	12%
Calcium:	26 mg	Polyunsaturated fat:	3%
Potassium:	543 mg	Cholesterol:	101 mg
Fiber:	0 gm	Sodium:	85 mg

Pork Stir-fry

Serves 4
15 Minutes

If you thought pork is high in fat and calories, try this recipe and look at the nutritional percentages!

16	ounces lean pork loin	1	teaspoon honey
1	teaspoon soy sauce, low sodium	1/2	cup pineapple juice
1	teaspoon worchestershire sauce,	1	teaspoon rosemary
	low sodium	1/4	teaspoon pepper
3/4	cup pineapple, fresh or canned	1	tablespoon parsley

Trim the pork of all visible fat. Cut the pork into bite-size pieces.

Saute the pork in a large skillet coated with cooking spray. Stir in the soy sauce, worchestershire sauce, pineapple, honey and juice. Season with rosemary, pepper and parsley.

Stir-fry for 2-3 minutes.

Nutrition information per serving: Calories: 171

Complex carbohydrates:	22%	Fat:	27%
Protein:	44%	Saturated fat:	10%
Iron:	1 mg	Monounsaturated fat:	13%
Calcium:	14 mg	Polyunsaturated fat:	4%
Potassium:	311 mg	Cholesterol:	53 mg
Fiber:	0 gm	Sodium:	104 mg

DESSERTS

Elegant Fruit Dessert

Serves 4
15 Minutes

This dessert is so easy and yet pretty enough to serve to company. It has lots of complex carbohydrates and fiber and is so good.

1	cup strawberries	1	tablespoon honey
1	cup blueberries	2	tablespoon brandy
1	cup peaches or pineapple	2	tablespoon lemon juice
1	cup kiwi	2	tablespoons streusel recipe topping (pg.95)

Use all of the fruits or a combination of your favorites. Slice fruit in bite-size pieces.

Mix the honey, brandy and lemon juice together. Toss the fruit in this mixture and spoon into individual serving bowls. Sprinkle each with 1/2 tablespoon of streusel topping (or you may prefer vanilla yogurt).

Nutrition information per serving: Calories: 169

Complex carbohydrates:	55%	Fat:	17%
Protein:	5%	Saturated fat:	2%
Iron:	1 mg	Monounsaturated fat;	9%
Calcium:	64 mg	Polyunsaturated fat:	6%
Potassium:	439 mg	Cholesterol:	0 mg
Fiber:	5 gm	Sodium:	25 mg

Souffle Almondine

Serves 6
45 Minutes
(20 M Preparation)

The smooth, rich flavor of this elegant dessert is surprisingly low in fat and high in calcium and potassium. Serve it with fruit or it is great by itself.

1/2	cup flour	1	cup egg substitute
1	teaspoon Sweet 'n Low	3	tablespoons Butter Buds
1/8	salt	3	tablespoons hot water
1/2	cup cold skim milk	1/3	cup almonds
2	cups scalded milk	6	egg whites
1	teaspoon almond extract	3/4	cup strawberries

Combine flour, Sweet 'n low and salt. Stir in the milk with a whisk. Scald 2 cups of milk and gradually add the hot milk to the flour mixture. Heat over low heat until thick, while stirring.

Mix the Butter Buds with the hot water. Beat the liquid butter with the extract and egg substitute. Cool. In a separate bowl, whip the egg whites until lightly stiff.

Gently fold the egg whites into the mixture. Pour this into a souffle dish coated with cooking spray. Bake at 350 degrees for 25 minutes.

Serve with fruit.

Nutrition information per serving:

Calories: 139

Complex carbohydrates:	43%	Fat:	25%
Protein:	29%	Saturated fat:	3%
Iron:	1mg	Monounsaturated fat:	16%
Calcium:	177 mg	Polyunsaturated fat:	6%
Potassium:	348 mg	Cholesterol:	2 mg
Fiber:	1 gm	Sodium:	197 mg

Frozen Chocolate Mousse

Serves 8
2 Hours (to chill)
(30 M Preparation)

The original of this recipe has been my favorite for years. It is very rich and smooth. This version is close to the original taste without the cholesterol, fat or calories.

21/2	tablespoons sugar	2	tablespoons margarine
2	teaspoons Sweet 'n Low	2	teaspoons Sweet 'n Low
1	cup egg substitute	3	tablespoons strong decaffeinated
2	tablespoons cognac or brandy		coffee
2	tablespoons chocolate chips	1/4	cup Butter Buds
1/4	cup cocoa	1/4	cup hot water
1	teaspoon canola oil	4	egg whites

Over simmering water, heat the sugar, Sweet 'n Low and egg substitute, beating constantly until thick. Add the liquor. Set the pan in a pan of ice water to cool.

Again, over simmering water, melt the chocolate chips, cocoa, oil, margarine, Sweet 'n Low and coffee, stirring frequently. Mix the Butter Buds and hot water and add to the chocolate mixture. Heat until the mixture is smooth. Combine with the egg mixture.

Beat the egg whites until stiff. Gently fold the egg whites into the chocolate mixture and pour into a souffle dish coated with cooking spray. (Any porcelain dish will do, or you may want to use individual serving dishes.) Freeze, covered, for 11/2hours or more.

Nutrition information per serving: Calories: 166

Complex carbohydrates:	15%	Fat:	34%
Protein:	25%	Saturated fat:	11%
Iron:	2 mg	Monounsaturated fat:	13%
Calcium:	32 mg	Polyunsaturated fat:	10%
Potassium:	256 mg	Cholesterol:	0 mg
Fiber:	2 gm	Sodium:	244 mg

*Original recipe information per serving: Calories: 248

Complex carbohydartes:	3%	Fat:	61%
Protein:	9%	Saturated fat:	35%
		Cholesterol:	156 mg

Apricot Mousse

Serves 6 (1/2 cup servings)
1 Hour
(30 M Preparation)

This is can be a dessert or a snack. The fruit content makes it sweet and nutrient rich.

11/2	cups dried apricots	1/2	cup skim milk
3/4	cup water	1/4	cup non-fat dry milk
1	tablespoon sugar	1/4	teaspoon vanilla extract
2	tablespoons water	1/2	tablespoon sugar
2	egg whites	1/2	teaspoon Sweet 'n Low
	1	teaspoon cinnamon sugar		

Combine the apricots and water and heat in a microwave on medium heat for 5 minutes. The apricots will be soft enough to mash easily. (Do not drain the water) Mash by hand or in a food processor.

Heat the sugar and water until thick. Set aside. Beat the egg whites until stiff. Gradually add the sugar syrup, while beating. Gently fold in the apricot mixture. Set aside.

Combine the milk, dry milk, sugar and Sweet 'n Low. Beat until stiff then fold this into the apricot mixture. Pour into a mold or individual serving bowls sprayed with cooking spray. Top with cinnamon sugar. Cover and freeze for at least 30 minutes or more.

Nutrition information per serving: Calories: 153

Complex carbohydrates:	72%	Fat:	0%
Protein:	13%	Saturated fat:	0%
Iron:	2 mg	Monounsaturated fat:	0%
Calcium:	109 mg	Polyunsaturated fat:	0%
Potassium:	741 mg	Cholesterol:	1 mg
Fiber:	4 gm	Sodium:	58 mg

Peach Tapioca

For a quick, great-tasting dessert try this one. Select whatever fruit is your favorite!

3	tablespoons tapioca, quick-cook	1	teaspoon vanilla
2 3/4	cups skim milk	2	teaspoons sugar
1/4	cup egg substitute	3/4	cup peaches, fresh or frozen

In a saucepan, combine tapioca and milk. Let stand 5 minutes. Add egg substitute, vanilla and sugar. Cook over medium heat, stirring occasionally to a full boil.

Remove from the stove (the tapioca thickens when it cools). Stir in the peaches (if frozen, be sure to thaw first). Pour into a glass or porcelain bowl and chill at least 30 minutes.

Nutrition information per serving: Calories: 77

Complex carbohydrates:	60%	Fat:	2%
Protein:	26%	Saturated fat:	1%
Iron:	0 mg	Monounsaturated fat:	1%
Calcium:	143 mg	Polyunsaturated fat:	0%
Potassium:	252 mg	Cholesterol:	2 mg
Fiber:	0 gm	Sodium:	72 mg

Chocolate-Raspberry Brownies

Makes 30 Squares
45 Minutes
(20 M Preparation)

These brownies are moist and rich. The raspberries add a wonderful flavor. Enjoy them plain or with our "Ice Cream" Icing (use 1/2 icing recipe and add 10 calories to each brownie).

2	tablespoons margarine		1/2	cup sugar
4	tablespoons cocoa		5	teaspoons Sweet 'n Low
1	tablespoon canola oil		1	teaspoon almond extract
1	cup egg substitute		1	cup flour
1	egg white		6	ounces raspberries, fresh or frozen
1/4	teaspoon salt			

Melt the margarine over low heat in a saucepan. Gradually add the cocoa and oil. Set aside.

With a mixer, beat the egg substitute, egg white and salt. To the egg mixture, add the sugar, Sweet 'n low and extract. Combine with the cocoa mixture.

Add the flour, beating with a whisk. Gently fold in the raspberries. Pour into a 9"x13" or a 10" square baking pan coated with cooking spray. Bake at 350 degrees for 25-30 minutes until done.

Nutrition information per square: Calories: 43

Complex carbohydrates:	39%	Fat:	20%
Protein:	12%	Saturated fat:	3%
Iron:	0 mg	Monounsaturated fat:	5%
Calcium:	12 mg	Polyunsaturated fat:	12%
Potassium:	50 mg	Cholesterol:	0 mg
Fiber:	1 gm	Sodium:	43 mg

*Original recipe information per square: Calories: 126

Complex carbohydrates:	25%	Fat:	40%
Protein:	8%	Saturated fat:	28%
		Cholesterol:	40 mg

COOKIES, CAKES AND PIES

Peanut Butter Cookies

Makes 60 small cookies
40 Minutes
(15 M Preparation)

Peanut butter is a good source of plant protein. The fat content is a bit higher than we prefer, but is nearly all monunsaturated and polyunsaturated. These cookies taste great and have a light texture.

3/4	cup sugar	2	cups peanut butter, natural,
1	teaspoon Sweet 'n Low		no oil or salt added
		4	egg whites

Mix the peanut butter, sugar and sweetener. With a mixer, beat the egg whites until stiff. Gently fold the egg whites into the peanut butter mixture.

Drop by spoonfuls onto a cookie sheet coated with cooking spray. Bake at 325 degrees for 25 minutes. Cool on a rack.

Nutrition information per cookie: Calories: 55

Complex carbohydrates:	14%	Fat:	61%
Protein:	18%	Saturated fat:	12%
Iron:	0 mg	Monounsaturated fat:	30%
Calcium:	3 mg	Polyunsaturated fat:	19%
Potassium:	55 mg	Cholesterol:	0 mg
Fiber:	1 gm	Sodium:	5 mg

Buttery Sugar Cookies

Makes 46 small cookies
30 Minutes
(20 M Preparation)

Can you believe these are sugar cookies you can have? These cookies have been modified, while maintaining the rich taste. They are not as high in sugar as the original recipe, but still do contain sugar, so please try not to eat too many at one time.

11/2	cups flour	1/3	cup Butter Buds
1/4	cup sugar	1	tablespoon hot water
1/2	teaspoon Sweet 'n Low	1	egg white
1/2	teaspoon baking powder	1/2	teaspoon vanilla extract
1/8	teaspoon salt	2	tablespoon egg substitute
2	tablespoons margarine, low fat	1	tablespoon half & half
	2	tablespoons sugar, for topping		

Combine the flour, sugar, Sweet & Low, baking powder and salt. Cut in the margarine. Combine the Butter Buds and hot water. Add this to the flour mixture. Add the egg white, vanilla, egg substitute and half & half.

Roll out on a floured surface to 1/8" thick and cut into desired shapes. Place on a non-stick cookie sheet coated with cooking spray.

Sprinkle each cookie lightly with sugar. Bake at 400 degrees for 10-12 minutes. Remove while warm and cool on racks.

Nutrition information per cookie: Calories: 22

Complex carbohydrates:	55%	Fat:	13%
Protein:	10%	Saturated fat:	3%
Iron:	0 %	Monounsaturated fat:	4%
Calcium:	9 %	Polyunsaturated fat:	6%
Potassium:	21 mg	Cholesterol:	0 mg
Fiber:	0 gm	Sodium:	18 mg

*Original recipe information per cookie: Calories: 51

Complex carbohydrates:	22%	Fat:	39%
Protein:	10%	Saturated fat:	25%
Sodium:	5 mg	Cholesterol:	9 mg

196

Linzer Cookies

● ●

Makes 24 cookies
35 Minutes
(25 M Preparation)

Linzer cookies have a buttery taste with the accent of spices for a european flavor. You may try substituting your favorite jam for the raspberry.

1	recipe for Buttery Sugar Cookies pg. 196	1/2	teaspoon cinnamon
		1/4	teaspoon nutmeg
4	tablespoons almonds	1/2	cup raspberry jam, low calorie

Make the Buttery Sugar Cookie recipe using 1 cup white flour and 1/2 cup wheat flour. Mix in the almonds and spices. Roll out to 1/8" thickness on a floured surface.

When cutting the rounds, make a small hole in the center of 1/2 of the rounds. Place the regular rounds on cookie sheet sprayed with cooking spray. Spread each of the rounds with 1 teaspoon of jam. Top them with the "holed" round.

Bake at 400 degrees for 10-12 minutes.

Nutrition information per cookie: Calories: 65

Complex carbohydrates:	50%	Fat:	9%
Protein:	9%	Saturated fat:	3%
Iron:	0 mg	Monunsaturated fat:	9%
Calcium:	19 mg	Polyunsaturated fat:	7%
Potassium:	71 mg	Cholesterol:	0 mg
Fiber:	1 gm	Sodium:	40 mg

Chocolate Chip Cookies

Makes 36
30 Minutes
(20 M preparation)

These cookies taste as good as the original recipe and are much better for you. They are so good, be careful not to eat too many!

1/4	cup sugar	1/2	teaspoon vanilla extract
3	tablespoons brown sugar	1	cup flour
1/2	teaspoon Sweet 'n Low	1/8	teaspoon salt
1/3	cup margarine, low fat	1/8	teaspoon baking soda
1	egg white	1/4	cup semi-sweet chocolate chips
1/4	cup egg substitute		

In a medium bowl, combine the sugars, Sweet 'n Low and margarine. Lightly beat the egg white, combining with the egg substitute and vanilla extract, then add to the sugar mixture.

In a separate bowl, sift together the flour, salt and baking soda. Add the sugar mixture to the flour mixture. Stir in the chocolate chips.

Drop by spoonfuls onto a cookie sheet coated with cooking spray. Bake at 350 degrees for 10 to 12 minutes.

Nutrition information per cookie: Calories: 34

Complex carbohydrates:	32%	Fat:	26%
Protein:	8%	Saturated fat:	9%
Iron:	0 mg	Monounsturated fat:	8%
Calcium:	7 mg	Polyunsaturated fat:	9%
Potassium:	17 mg	Cholesterol:	0 mg
Fiber:	0 gm	Sodium:	32 mg

*Original recipe information per cookie: Calories: 57

Complex carbohydrates:	21%	Fat:	43%
Protein:	7%	Saturated fat:	26%

Chocolate Almond Cookies

Makes 44 Small Cookies
40 Minutes
(15 M Preparation)

These cookies are wonderfully rich with a light taste.

4	egg whites	1	teaspoon Sweet 'n Low
1/2	teaspoon cream of tartar	1/2	cup cocoa
1/4	cup sugar	1/2	teaspoon almond extract
2	tablespoon powdered sugar	1/3	cup sliced almonds

In a large bowl, beat the egg whites and cream of tartar with a mixer until stiff. Add sugars and sweetener gradually while beating. Continue beating and add cocoa and extract. Fold in the almonds.

Drop by spoonfuls onto cookie sheets coated with cooking spray. Bake at 325 degrees for 25 minutes until crisp. Remove from the sheets while warm and cool on a rack.

Nutrition information per cookie: Calories: 16

Complex carbohydrates:	16%	Fat:	34 %
Protein:	18%	Saturated fat:	7 %
Iron:	0 mg	Monounsaturated fat:	21%
Calcium:	5 mg	Polyunsaturated fat:	6 %
Potassium:	29 mg	Cholesterol:	0 mg
Fiber:	1 gm	Sodium:	8 mg

"Ice Cream" Icing

Serves 10 (2 tablespoon servings)
15 Minutes

The original of this recipe came from my mother and has been my favorite for years. We call it "Ice Cream" icing because when the dessert is chilled, the icing tastes like ice cream!

1	tablespoon margarine, low fat	1	tablespoon canola oil
1	tablespoon flour	3	tablespoons sugar
1	tablespoon cornstarch	2	teaspoons Sweet 'n Low
1/2	cup skim milk	1	teaspoon vanilla extract
3	tablespoons Butter Buds	5	tablespoons cocoa
3	tablespoons hot water		

In a sauce pan, combine the margarine, flour and cornstarch. While beating with a whisk, add the milk gradually and cook over low heat. Stir regularly.

In a separate bowl, beat the Butter Buds and hot water together. Then beat in the oil, sugar, sweetener, vanilla and cocoa. Add to the flour mixture and continue beating with a whisk over low heat until smooth. Cool and use to frost cakes or brownies. Chill.

Nutrition information per serving: Calories: 54

Complex carbohydrates:	28%	Fat:	38%
Protein:	8%	Saturated fat:	9%
Iron:	0mg	Monounsaturated fat:	15%
Calcium:	14 mg	Polyunsaturated fat:	14%
Potassium:	63 mg	Cholesterol:	0 mg
Fiber:	1 gm	Sodium:	35 mg

*Original recipe infromation per serving: Calories: 85

Fat:	54%
Saturated fat:	36%

Chocolate-Strawberry Torte

Serves 12
2 Hours
(35 M Preparation)

There's nothing better with chocolate than fruit. This torte is so rich, all you need is one piece.

1	cup vanilla yogurt, low fat	11/4	cup flour
1/4	cup crushed strawberries	1/4	cup cocoa
2	tablespoons Butter Buds	1/4	teaspoon baking soda
2	tablespoons margarine, low fat	1/4	teaspoon baking powder
1/3	cup sugar	1/2	cup plain yogurt, non-fat
1	teaspoon Sweet 'n Low	1/3	cup strawberry preserves, low-cal.
2	egg whites	1/2	recipe "Ice Cream" Icing, pg. 200
1/2	teaspoon vanilla extract		

Mix the yogurt and strawberries together. Line an 8" cake pan with wax paper. Spread the yogurt mixture onto the wax paper. Freeze 2 hours.

Soften the margarine and mix with the Butter Buds. Gradually add the sugar, Sweet 'n Low, egg whites and extract. In a separate bowl, combine the flour, cocoa, baking soda and baking powder. Then add the sugar mixture and yogurt. Pour batter into an 8" cake pan coated with cooking spray. Bake at 350 degrees for 30 minutes.

When done, turn out onto a rack and cool. Carefully cut the cake into two layers. Place the bottom layer on a serving plate. Place the frozen yogurt on the bottom layer and spread with the preserves. Top with the second cake layer. Drizzle the top with icing. Cover and serve immediately or keep in freezer. (It should keep 3-5 days without drying out)

Nutrition information per slice: Calories: 135

Complex carbohydrates:	44%	Fat:	14%
Protein:	12%	Saturated fat:	4%
Iron:	4 mg	Monounsaturated fat:	6%
Calcium:	89 mg	Polyunsaturated fat:	5%
Potassium:	163 mg	Cholesterol:	1 mg
Fiber:	1 gm	Sodium:	96 mg

Rich Chocolate Cake

Serves 10
1 Hour
(20 M Preparation)

If you like chocolate, you will love the rich, moist taste of this cake. (The fat percentage appears high, but is mostly monounsaturated) The nutrition information includes the icing, but try the cake without the icing for lower fat and sugar percentages.

2	cups flour		Dash of salt
1/2	sugar	1/2	cup canola oil
1/3	cup cocoa	1	cup skim milk
1	teaspoon Sweet 'n Low	1/2	cup brewed decaffeinated coffee
2	teaspoons baking soda	1	tablespoon brandy
	1/2 recipe "Ice Cream" Icing, pg. 200		

Sift the flour, sugar, cocoa, sweetener, baking soda and salt together. Gradually add the oil, milk, coffee and brandy. Beat with a whisk until smooth.

Pour into a 9" cake pan coated with cooking spray. Bake at 350 degrees for 40-45 minutes. When done, turn onto a rack to cool. Spread with the icing. For best flavor, cover and keep chilled.

Nutrition information per slice: Calories: 235

Complex carbohydrates:	34%	Fat:	43%
Protein:	7%	Saturated fat:	4%
Iron:	1 mg	Monounsaturated fat:	25%
Calcium:	75 mg	Polyunsaturated fat:	13%
Potassium:	138 mg	Cholesterol:	0 mg
Fiber:	2 gm	Sodium:	187 mg

*Original recipe information per slice: Calories: 440

Complex carbohydrates:	17%	Fat:	37%
Protein:	5%	Saturated fat:	15%
Added sugar:	47%	Cholesterol:	90 mg

Berry Cheesecake

Serves 8
1 Hour
(15 M Preparation)

Choose the your favorite berries for this cheesecake. It tastes as rich as the original version. It's great served by itself or try a little of the "Chocolate Sauce" on it.

11/2	cup crushed graham crackers (preferably oat bran)	1	tablepoon cornstarch
3	tablespoons Butter Buds	1/2	cup egg substitute
3	tablepoons hot water	1	egg white
1/2	teaspoon almond extract	1	cup strawberries, raspberries <u>or</u> blueberries
2	cups plain "Yogurt Cream Cheese", pg.97		

Mix the Butter Buds with the hot water. Add the crushed graham crackers and press into a 9" pie pan coated with cooking spray. Set aside.

In a medium bowl, combine the yogurt cream cheese, cornstarch, extract, egg substitute and egg white, stirring gently. Fold in the berries.

Pour into the pie pan coated with the crackers. Bake at 325 degrees for 45-50 minutes. Cool. Chill in refrigerator.

Nutrition information per slice: Calories: 100

Complex carbohydrates:	45%	Fat:	14%
Protein:	23%	Saturated fat:	5%
Iron:	1 mg	Monounsaturated fat:	4%
Calcium:	118 mg	Polyunsaturated fat:	5%
Potassium:	226 mg	Cholesterol:	3 mg
Fiber:	1 gm	Sodium:	131 mg

Apple-Spice Cake

Serves 10
1 1/2 Hour
(40 M Preparation)

This is a dense, moist cake similar to a coffee cake, but faster!

1	cup flour	1/4	cup sugar
1/2	teaspooon baking powder	1/4	cup brown sugar
1/2	teaspoon baking soda	1	teaspoon Sweet 'n Low
1/4	teaspooon salt	1/4	cup margarine, low fat
1/2	tablespoon cinnamon	1/4	cup egg substitute
1/2	teaspoon allspice	1/2	teaspoon vanilla extract
1/2	teaspoon nutmeg	1/2	cup plain yogurt, non-fat
1/4	ginger	1/4	cup oat bran
1/4	teaspoon cloves	1	apple, peeled and sliced

1   recipe streusel topping, pg. 95

Sift together the flour, baking powder, baking soda, salt and spices. In a separate bowl, gradually add the sugars and sweetener to the margarine. Beat at high speed of the mixer until light and fluffy. At medium speed, beat in the egg substitute. Add the vanilla and yogurt, beating at low speed, adding the oat bran.

Gradually add the flour mixture. Coarsely chop the apple in a food processor and add to the mixture. Pour into a non-stick cake pan coated with cooking spray. Bake at 350 degrees for 40-45 minutes.

When cake is done, let stand 10 minutes, then turn out and cool on a rack. Sprinkle with the streusel topping while still warm.

Nutrition information per slice:

Calories: 146

Complex carbohydrates:	37%	Fat:	23%
Protein:	8%	Saturated fat:	4%
Iron:	2 mg	Monounsaturated fat:	10%
Calcium:	86 mg	Polyunsaturated fat:	9%
Potassium:	310 mg	Cholesterol:	0 mg
Fiber:	2 gm	Sodium:	140 mg

Pie Crust

Most pie crusts are made with butter or shortening which are very high in fat. The substitutions in this recipe still allow a light, flakey taste with much lower fat and saturated fat.

3/4	cup white flour	1/4	cup maragrine, low fat
1/4	cup wheat flour	11/2	tablespoons cold water
1/4	teaspoon salt		

Sift the flours and salt together. Cut in the margarine and add water to desired consistency. The dough should be crumbly. Form into a ball and roll to 1/8" thickness.

Place in a 9" pie pan and flute the edges. Bake at 400 degrees for 10 minutes, if recipe requires a pre-baked crust.

Nutrition information per slice:
Calories: 75

Complex carbohydrates:	57%	Fat:	35%
Protein:	8%	Saturated fat:	6%
Iron:	1 mg	Monounsaturated fat:	11%
Calcium:	25 mg	Polyunsaturated fat:	18%
Potassium:	21 mg	Cholesterol:	0 mg
Fiber:	1 gm	Sodium:	92 mg

*Original recipe nutrition per slice:
Calories: 113

Complex carbohydrates:	19%	Fat:	56%
Protein:	6%	Saturated fat:	15%

Apple Pie

Serves 8
11/2 Hour
(30 M Preparation)

The "All-American" apple pie is a healthy dessert everyone loves. Here is a version with lower fat . If you like yours with ice cream, try frozen yogurt or ice milk.

2	recipes pie crust, pg. 205	2	tablespoons flour
1/3	cup sugar	6	cups apples, peeled, sliced thin
11/2	teaspoon Sweet 'n Low	2	tablespoons margarine, low fat
1	teaspoon cinnamon	Dash of cinnamon sugar	
1/8	teaspoon salt		

Make the pie crust recipes, divide in half and roll each out to 1/8" thickness. Place one in a 9" pie pan.

In a large bowl, combine the sugar, Sweet 'n Low, spices, flour and apples. Spoon into the pie pan. Dot with margarine. Place the second crust on top either whole or in a lattice-work pattern, fluting the edges. Sprinkle the top with the cinnamon sugar.

Bake at 450 degrees for 15 minutes. Then lower the oven to 375 degrees for 45-50 minutes.

Nutrition information per slice: Calories: 238

Complex carbohydrates:	50%	Fat:	29%
Protein:	4%	Saturated fat:	5%
Iron:	1 mg	Monounsaturated fat:	10%
Calcium:	18 mg	Polyunsaturated fat:	14%
Potassium:	259 mg	Cholesterol:	0 mg
Fiber:	3 gm	Sodium:	229 mg

*Original recipe information per slice: Calories: 304

Complex carbohydrates:	34%	Fat:	37%
Protein:	5%	Saturated fat:	13%
Sugar:	25%	Sodium:	357 mg

Peach-Blueberry Pie

Serves 8
1 1/2 Hour
(25 M Preparation)

Combination fruit pies are a great way to have a healthy dessert. If fresh fruit is not available, frozen will work just as well.

1	pie crust recipe, pg. 205		2	teaspoons Sweet 'n Low
1/2	cup egg substitute		2	cups peaches, sliced
2	tablespoons cornstarch		1	cup blueberries
1/3	cup sugar		1	recipe streusel topping, pg. 95

Make the pie crust recipe. Roll out to 1/8" thick. Press into 9" pie pan. Bake at 300 degrees for 10 minutes. (This helps prevent a soggy crust)

Combine the egg substitutes, cornstarch, sugar, Sweet 'n Low and fruit. Pour into pie shell. Bake at 400 degrees for 15 minutes, then at 300 degrees for 30 minutes. Make the streusel recipe and sprinkle over the top of the fruit. Bake for 10 minutes more.

Nutrition information per slice: Calories: 171

Complex carbohydrates:	45%	Fat:	23%
Protein:	7%	Saturated fat:	4%
Iron:	1%	Monounsaturated fat:	10%
Calcium:	21 mg	Polyunsturated fat:	10%
Potassium:	230 mg	Cholesterol:	0 mg
Fiber:	2 gm	Sodium:	129 mg

*Original recipe information per slice: Calories: 405

Complex carbohydrates:	28%	Fat:	35%
Protein:	20%	Saturated fat:	14%
Sodium:	285 mg	Cholesterol:	72 mg

Strawberry Rhubarb Pie

Serves 8
1 1/2 Hour
(25 M Preparation)

This pie is a wonderful balance of sweet and tart.

2	recipes for pie crust, pg. 203	2	teaspoons Sweet 'n Low
2	cups strawberries	2	tablespoons cornstarch
2	cups rhubarb, fresh or frozen	2	teaspoons margarine, low fat
1/3	cup sugar	1/8	teaspoon cinnamon
2	teaspoon Sweet 'n Low		

Mix together the fruit, sugar, sweetener and cornstarch in a glass or porcelain bowl. Let stand for 15 minutes.

Make the pie crust recipe, divide in half and roll each out to 1/8" thickness. Press one crust into a 9" pie pan; do not flute the edges. Cut the other pie crust into 1" strips and and set aside.

Pour the fruit mixture into the pie shell, dot with margarine and sprinkle with cinnamon. Lay the crust strips in a lattice-work pattern across the top of the pie, sealing the edges by fluting.

Nutrition information per slice: Calories: 164

Complex carbohydrates:	46%	Fat;	30%
Protein:	5 %	Saturated fat:	5 %
Iron:	1 mg	Monounstaurated fat:	11%
Calcium:	42 mg	Polyunsaturated fat:	14%
Potassium:	451 mg	Cholesterol:	0 mg
Fiber:	2 gm	Sodium:	318 mg

*Original recipe information per slice: Calories: 240

Complex carbohydrates:	34%	Fat:	34%
Protein:	4%	Saturated fat:	13%
		Cholesterol:	15 mg

Pumpkin Pie

Serves 8
11/2 Hour
(30 M Preparation)

Pumpkin pie is one of our favorites. It's great warm or cold, but especially warm in the winter. Try it with the Whipped Topping *on page 98.*

1	recipe for pie crust, pg. 205	1	teaspoon cinnamon
1	16 ounce can pumpkin	1/2	teaspoon allspice
1	12 ounce can evaporated	1/2	cup egg substitute
	skim milk	1	egg white
1/4	cup brown sugar	1/4	teaspoon nutmeg
1	tablespoon Brown Sugar Twin	1/8	teaspoon cloves
2	teaspoons Sweet 'n Low	1/2	teaspoon ginger
1/4	teapsoon salt		

Make the pie crust, place in a 9" pie pan and set aside.

Whip the pumpkin and the milk with a whisk. Add in the sugars, sweeteners, salt and spices. In a separate bowl, beat the egg white and egg substitute, then add to the pumpkin mixture.

Pour the mixture into the pie shell. Bake at 425 degrees for 15 minutes. Then lower the oven to 350 degrees and bake 45 minutes more.

Nutrition information per slice: Calories: 119

Complex carbohydrates:	44%	Fat:	18%
Protein:	18%	Saturated fat:	4%
Iron:	1 mg	Monounsaturated fat:	6%
Calcium:	132 mg	Polyunsaturated fat:	8%
Potassium:	395 mg	Cholesterol:	1 mg
Fiber:	1 gm	Sodium:	263 mg

Chocolate Pie

Serves 8
1 1/4 Hour
(45 M Preparation)

The original recipe for this pie has a rich, creamy taste that is still true in this version. Try it with the Whipped Topping on page 98.

1	recipe pie crust, pg. 95	1/2	cup sugar
21/4	cups skim milk	1	teaspoons Sweet 'n Low
1/4	cup nonfat dry milk	1	teaspooon instant coffee
1/4	cup water	3/4	cup egg substitute
1/4	cup cocoa	2	tablespoons Butter Buds
1/2	tablespoon canola oil	1	tablespoon margarine, low fat
1/4	cup flour	1/8	teaspoon almond extract
1/4	teaspoon salt	2	teaspoons vanilla extract
1/4	cup skim milk		

Make the pie crust recipe, roll out to 1/8" thick and press into a 9" pie pan. Bake at 400 degrees for 10 minutes.

Heat the milk until scalded. Mix the water and dry milk and add to the milk. Add the cocoa and oil. In a separate bowl mix the flour with the milk, sugar, salt, Sweet 'n Low and coffee with a whisk. Add this to the cocoa mixture. Cook over low heat 15 minutes, stirring occasionally with the whisk until smooth.

Gradually add the egg substitute to the cocoa mixture. Cook 3 minutes. Add the Butter Buds, margarine and extracts. Cook 1 minute more. Pour into the pie shell. Bake at 325 degrees for 30 minutes.

Nutrition information per slice: Calories: 162

Complex carbohydrates:	42%	Fat:	20%
Protein:	18%	Saturated fat:	4%
Iron:	1 mg	Monounsaturated fat:	5%
Calcium:	143 mg	Polyunsaturated fat:	10%
Potassium:	243 mg	Cholesterol:	2 mg
Fiber:	1 gm	Sodium:	270 mg

*Original recipe nutrition per slice: Calories: 287

Complex carbohydrates:	28%	Fat:	34%
Protein:	15%	Saturated fat:	14%
Sodium:	345 gm	Cholesterol:	112 mg

210

Recommended Reading

THE EIGHT-WEEK CHOLESTEROL CURE COOKBOOK,
> Robert E. Kowalski. Harper & Row, Publishers, Inc., 1989

THE AMERICAN HEART ASSOCIATION LOW-FAT, LOW-CHOLES-TEROL COOKBOOK,
> Scott Grundy, M.D., Ph.D., Editor. Random House, Inc., 1989

DON'T EAT YOUR HEART OUT COOKBOOK,
> Joseph C. Piscatella. New York: Workman Publishing, 1987

CHOICES FOR A HEALTHY HEART,
> Joseph C. Piscatella. New York: Workman Publishing, 1989

THE FITNESS BOOK,
> Bud Getchell. Indianapolis: Benchmark Press, Inc., 1987

EATER'S CHOICE,
> R. Goor and N. Goor. New York: Houghton Mifflin Co., 1987

CONTROLLING CHOLESTEROL,
> Kenneth Cooper. New York: Bantam Books, 1988

THE NEW AMERICAN DIET,
> Connor and Connor. New York: Simon and Schuster, 1986

INDEX

Source Notes

Nutrient values for HEALTHY *CUISINE* have been obtained from THE *DINE* ® *WINDOWS* : *Diet Improvement, Nutrient Evaluation Software Package,* DINE Systems, Inc., Five Bluebird Lane, West Amherst, New York 14228, (716) 688-2492; (716) 834-3463.

DINE ® Windows is a full featured, graphics-based nutrient analysis, diet improvement software package. A new book, *The DINE System* ®: *How To Improve Your Nutrition And Health,* written by Drs. Darwin and Kathryn Dennson, provides you with a free analysis (on a one-time basis) of your diet.

Information regarding *The Dine System* ®: *How To Improve Your Nutrition And Health* can be obtained from the above address and phone number.